ISBN 978-1-330-90869-3
PIBN 10120064

1 MONTH OF
FREE
READING

at

www.ForgottenBooks.com

By purchasing this book you are eligible for one month membership to ForgottenBooks.com, giving you unlimited access to our entire collection of over 700,000 titles via our web site and mobile apps.

To claim your free month visit:

www.forgottenbooks.com/free120064

British Regiments in War and Peace

II

THE NORTHUMBERLAND FUSILIERS

The Badge of the Northumberland Fusiliers.

THE
NORTHUMBERLAND
FUSILIERS

BY

WALTER WOOD

AUTHOR OF 'WITH THE FLAG AT SEA,' ETC.

ILLUSTRATED

LONDON
GRANT RICHARDS

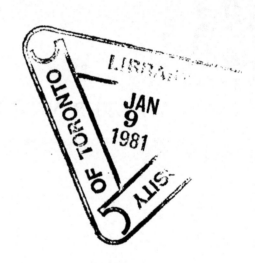

TO

THE OFFICERS

NON-COMMISSIONED OFFICERS

AND MEN

OF

THE NORTHUMBERLAND FUSILIERS

INTRODUCTION

SIXTEEN battle-honours on the colours of the
" Ever-fighting, Never-failing Fifth " stand for
what the Northumberland Fusiliers have done
for Crown and country.   But those distinctions,
illustrious and wide-reaching though they are,
do not go beyond indicating part of the
regiment's work.   They cannot do more than
that, because the first of the honours dates only
from the year 1762, whereas the regiment has
existed, and has been almost constantly in action,
for more than two centuries and a quarter.

The Fifth began well, for very soon after
they were raised they lost nearly half their
officers and men.   This was at the siege of
Maestricht, in Holland.   In two more years—
at St. Denis—the regiment again suffered heavily,
losing 12 officers and 50 men killed, and over

b

100 wounded. The Fifth led the attack in the most valiant style, and the French were routed. For years the regiment fought in Flanders, afterwards in Portugal, then at Gibraltar during the siege of 1727; later in France and Germany. In the last-named country it secured its first and most famous honour—" Wilhelmstahl," for that honour is not only not shared by any other regiment in the British Army, but it also made the Fifth the first British grenadier regiment, and gave them other unique distinctions. At Wilhelmstahl the Fifth took more than twice their number of French grenadiers prisoners, and finally helped to capture nearly a whole French division. An act so exceptional demanded unusual recognition, and accordingly the Fifth were allowed for many years to wear French grenadier caps, instead of the hat in ordinary use by the British troops of the day.

To this famous privilege there was quickly added another, which is as greatly cherished— that red and white hackle feather which is worn alone by the Northumberland Fusiliers, no other

British corps sharing the right to it. This plume was given to the regiment in recognition of its valour at St. Lucie in 1778. The regiment was furiously attacked by an army of 9000 Frenchmen; but the assailants were repulsed with the loss of 500 killed and 1100 wounded, the Fifth losing 15 killed and 130 wounded. For this notable victory the honour was gained of wearing a plume in the head-dress, because on the field of battle the Fifth took from the dead Frenchmen plumes more than enough to decorate the whole regiment.

The Fifth Fusiliers have indeed a bewildering wealth of distinctions. Besides the unique honours of Wilhelmstahl, the plume, and of being the first British grenadier regiment, they rank as one of the oldest corps in the Line, and possess one of the most ancient badges and mottoes in our army—St. George and the Dragon, with *Quo fata vocant.* To the Fifth also belongs the distinction of establishing the first instance on record of a charge with the bayonet being made upon cavalry by infantry in line. Again, the Fifth enjoy the privilege of wearing red and white roses in the head-dress on St. George's Day—a very old custom, and so faithfully honoured that neither war nor distance is excuse for non-observance.   In the past year—1900—roses were sent from England to South Africa, where the officers and men of the regiment on active service stuck the flower in cap and helmet, and by means of it maintained a link with home six thousand miles away.

The device of England's patron saint is not borne by any regiment except the Fifth.   In the matter of facings, too, the Fifth are honoured. The colour is "gosling green," and it has for a lengthened period been one of the peculiarities of the dress of the regiment.   For a season the ancient privilege was tampered with, but representations made in the proper quarter have been successful, and the historic facings have been restored to the regiment and the *Army List*, to the great pride and satisfaction of the corps. This particular colour, which has been produced by one firm of Yorkshire dyers for more than a hundred years, is worn exclusively by the Fifth.   There is a further distinction, which may be almost called a literary one, for Scott, in *Waverley*, made the gallant conduct at Prestonpans of Charles Whitefoord, who subsequently became the colonel of the Fifth, the groundwork of one of the most striking scenes in the novel. To these and other matters further reference is made in the chapters of this volume.

The Fifth have enjoyed the right, very rare in the British Army, of possessing a third colour. The distinction arose, it is believed, out of the battle of Wilhelmstahl in 1762, and the third colour was possessed by the regiment until 1833. In that year, to the great grief of the Fifth, the colours, including the third, were destroyed by an accidental fire at Gibraltar. Strenuous efforts were made to get permission for the trophy to be replaced, but without success, and the regiment had to be content with permission, granted on May 14, 1836, for "Wilhelmstahl" to be borne on the colours. This third banner, which was small, and of green silk, was inscribed with the badge, motto, number, and designation of the corps, and was carried at the head of the regiment, amid the band and drummers. The distinction is supposed to have originated in the capture by the Fifth of the colours of the French Grenadiers at Wilhelmstahl, as well as the Grenadiers themselves.

The 1st and 2nd Battalions possess a third colour at the present day, subscribed for by the officers, and the newly-raised 3rd and 4th Battalions are making similar arrangements to provide themselves with a third colour. Those in possession of the 1st and 2nd Battalions are facsimiles of the old one. Each appears once a year only, on St. George's Day, when it is carried, as of old, amongst the drums. This is usually called " the third," or " drummers' colour."

Of the quickstep of the Fifth there is little more to say than that it is the same as the quickstep of other Fusilier Regiments—" The British Grenadiers." The Fifth share this march in common with the Royal Artillery, the Royal Engineers, the Grenadier Guards, and the other eight Fusilier Regiments in the British Army.

Of all these distinctions the Fifth are very proud, and justly so, for they shed peculiar lustre on the regiment; but there is another cause for great satisfaction with them, and that is their *esprit de corps.* This has been at all times one of the most marked characteristics of the regiment. It has been noted and referred to repeatedly by members of the Fifth themselves; but it has been commented upon also by men who have had no actual association with the regiment. Amongst these was Major Patterson, a Peninsular officer who was not of the Fifth, and who therefore spoke without prejudice. Probably in no other regiment in the British Army has this spirit been more evident and more carefully fostered than in the " Old and Bold." In the earlier years of the century it gave the Fifth an officer like Ridge, and at the close men like Keith-Falconer, " Young Ray," and " Boy Booth "—to name three only of that brave band who have gone to rest in South Africa. The spirit, too, is evidenced in every number of the regimental journal, the *St. George's Gazette,* one of the oldest, ablest, and most successful papers of its class, and the first to find its way to the Royal presence. In January 1897 an *édition de luxe* of a number of the journal was accepted by the late Queen. No issue of the paper can be read without proof appearing of the great, silent, inexpressible motive power which binds all ranks and sections of the Fifth together, and makes them not so much a mere regiment as that "band of brothers" spoken of by Nelson in relation to himself and fellow-officers.

Only recently an example was afforded of the way in which the regiment is remembered in the farthest corners of the world, and how, despite the passing of the years, the spirit of the corps remains with those who have been of its life and blood. A few years since, when the 1st Battalion was quartered at Cambridge Barracks, Woolwich, it was visited by Mr. Franklin, an old member who had left the regiment half a century ago. Eventually he accompanied the battalion on the march from Woolwich to Aldershot. On leaving he was presented with a complete uniform of the Fifth, including busby, to take back with him to his home in Australia. When he died it was found that he had left directions in his will for the sum of £50 to be expended on a treat to the children of the regiment—the love of which had never left him. It was this affection, too, which prompted the Militia battalion stationed at Malta to cable to the members of the Fifth who on St. George's Day 1900 were held by the fortune of war as prisoners at Pretoria, the one-word greeting, "Luck."

In 1886 the regiment came into possession of a historic relic through the kindness of Mrs. King, the widow of Captain John Wingfield King, 5th Fusiliers, who was shot on November 19, 1868, at an election disturbance in Sligo, when Deputy-Lieutenant of that county. Captain King was the son of Sir Henry King, K.C.B., who served many years with great distinction in the "Old and Bold." The relic was one of the original colour poles which were carried by the regiment in the Peninsular War. On the reduction of the 2nd Battalion in 1816, the colours were presented to its Colonel, Sir Henry King, who commanded it during the Peninsular

Campaign. At his death they became the property of his son, Captain King. Mrs. King presented to the Officers' Mess a small piece of the Queen's colour pole, which is now carefully preserved in a glass case, and she afterwards, in 1886, gave the pole which carried the old regimental colour, and which is in a very good state of preservation. It has been attached to the regimental colour now carried by the 1st Battalion, and bears the following inscription on a silver plate: "This pole was carried by the 5th Regiment during the Peninsular War, and in 1816 became the property of Sir Henry King, K.C.B., whose daughter-in-law, the widow of Captain John W. King, late of the 5th, graciously presented it to the 1st Battalion." The remnants of the original colours (of which the 1st Battalion has a small piece in a picture frame) are in the possession of Captain King's eldest son, at his residence in Australia. Mrs. King, who died in 1899, took the greatest interest in everything connected with the Fifth.

For a great many years the regiment possessed a highly-valued "Order of Merit." To this reference is made in Chapter III.; but it may be said here that so admirable were the results to the Fifth of the introduction of this reward that they suggested to the authorities the Long Service and Good Conduct Medal now in general use.

It is somewhat strange that in the two and a quarter centuries of the regiment's existence the senior battalions should have met only twice; it is still more singular that one station—Gibraltar—should have been the meeting-place each time. In 1800 the 1st and 2nd Battalions were quartered together at that fortress. In 1896 the 1st was at Gibraltar and the 2nd on passage home from Singapore on board the *Cephalonia.* On New Year's Eve the transport touched at the Rock, and accordingly the two battalions met. The officers, numbering thirty-nine, dined together at the Mess, and of this notable gathering a record was kept by each officer signing his name in the Mess Meeting Minute Book.

In the long period of its existence the regiment has naturally been the home of many

famous and noted people. Of these Colonel
Ridge, of immortal memory, Phœbe Hessel,
and Private James Grant may be named, Colonel
Ridge as representing all that has been excellent
in the higher ranks of the Fifth, Phœbe Hessel
as typifying the romance of the regiment, and
Grant as an example of that courage and devotion which have at all times marked the doings
of the corps on active service. Of the colonel
much is naturally written in succeeding pages.
Grant belonged to the 2nd Battalion of the
Fifth when in the Peninsula. As a member of
the band his duty was not so much in the front
as in the rear, but such was Grant's warlike
spirit that he could not keep himself out of
the fray. He invariably stole away from the
band when his regiment had gone into action,
and took to himself the arms of the first man
on the field who, by disablement, could not use
them. Grant was a tall and likely soldier, and
fell in on the right of the Grenadier Company
and fought until the end of the battle. Having
done that, he returned to the less exciting duties
of the bandsman. It is curious that although

Grant took part in some of the fiercest of the Peninsular fights he escaped without a wound. It is strange also that the death of a man like him should have been brought about by such a simple thing as a fall. Yet Grant died at Malta in 1835 from that cause. He had been appointed Sergeant-Major of the regiment in 1828. The Fifth erected to his memory a handsome tomb, on which a record of his achievements was placed.

Phœbe Hessel was a character famous not only in the annals of the Fifth but also in British military history generally. She was one of the most celebrated of the few women who have served as soldiers in the British Army. Born at Stepney in 1713, she dressed herself as a man and enlisted, at the age of fifteen years, in the Fifth, the regiment being at that time under orders for the West Indies. Phœbe's purpose was to follow and keep near her lover, Samuel Golding, who had accompanied his regiment, the 2nd Foot, now the Queen's (Royal West Surrey Regiment), to the West Indies. Eventually the 2nd Foot and the Fifth were

xx NORTHUMBERLAND FUSILIERS

quartered together at Gibraltar, where Golding was wounded and invalided home to Plymouth. After leaving the service Phœbe married Golding, and they lived happily for more than twenty years. Not long after her husband's death Mrs. Golding married a Brighton fisherman named William Hessel, who died about 1792. Phœbe, however, lived until December 12, 1821, having then reached the age of 108 years. It is related of her that before her decease she pathetically complained that every one could die except herself. She was buried in the churchyard of St. Nicholas, Brighton, and on a tombstone there the principal events of her remarkable life are set forth. "She served for many years," the inscription states, "as a private soldier in the 5th Regiment of Foot in different parts of Europe, and in the year 1745 fought under the Duke of Cumberland at the battle of Fontenoy, where she received a bayonet wound in her arm. Her long life, which commenced in the time of Queen Anne, extended to the reign of George IV., by whose munificence she received comfort and support in her latter years." A picture of the memorial is in the possession of the officers of the 2nd Battalion of the Fifth.

The Fifth have such a long and striking record of campaigning that it is only possible to obtain a clear record of their services by scanning tables of their fights and losses. I have accordingly prepared such statements, which are given in the Appendix, and in which, while the battles and sieges and their cost to the regiment can be seen at a glance, other details may be incorporated which would not only burden the narrative itself but also very probably escape attention.

As in the case of *The Rifle Brigade*, many authorities have been drawn upon for facts contained in this volume; but I am specially indebted to the editor of the *St. George's Gazette* (Major J. W. Malet) for placing at my disposal a complete file of that journal from 1883 to the end of 1900. The pages of that periodical contain a mass of information relating to the regiment which is not available in any other way, and which is original and to all intents and purposes unpublished.

Each British regiment has its own peculiar way of referring to itself, irrespective of the official designation in the *Army List*. The regiment dealt with in this volume knows itself as the Fifth, and that honoured name is used throughout these pages.

CONTENTS

ILLUSTRATIONS

CHAPTER I

THE EARLY YEARS OF THE REGIMENT

SINCE the Northumberland Fusiliers were raised more than two centuries and a quarter ago, they have held themselves in instant readiness to obey whatever orders have been given to them for fulfilment.   Those orders have been issued lavishly, and so it has happened that in all sorts of countries, and under all possible conditions, the Fifth have been concerned in war, and have earned a fighting reputation second to none in the Service.   That is saying a good deal, because the British Army includes some regiments which have a record of service unparalleled by that of any other military bodies in the world.   For sheer weight of fighting, the Old and Young Guards of Napoleon may not have been surpassed

B

by any other troops ; but their record covered a comparatively limited period, and their field of operations was restricted in comparison with that of British soldiers, for the demands of Empire have made the latter fight in every corner of the world, and during a very great length of time.

The regiment was raised for the Dutch service in 1674. In that year a treaty of peace was negotiated between England and Holland, and the Dutch Government, which had employed auxiliary British troops in former wars, and had found those soldiers of great service, obtained permission to have certain British regiments again in its pay. When, therefore, Charles II. in 1674 disbanded part of his army, many of the officers and men proceeded to Holland, and there the formation of a British division was begun. Rapid progress was made, and by the autumn the Prince of Orange, who was besieging Grave, in North Brabant, was informed that ten English and Irish companies, complete and fit for service, were 18 miles away. The Prince immediately ordered these troops to join him, and they did so, sharing in the siege. The capture of Grave on October 28 ended the campaign, and the troops went into quarters. During the winter four regiments of British subjects were formed—two English, one Scotch, and one Irish. This Irish corps became the Fifth—the Northumberland Fusiliers.

In 1675 the designation " Irish " was discontinued, and many English gentlemen received commissions in the regiment. The badge of St. George and the Dragon, with the motto *Quo fata vocant*, was resumed, and the facings of the uniform were gosling green. These two ancient distinctions remain with the Fifth exclusively to this day.

The new regiment had been in action already ; but it was soon to share in operations far more desperate than the siege of Grave. About two o'clock one morning in July 1676 the drums beat " To arms," and the regiment assembled at the alarm post and began a five days' march, which ended, to the enemy's astonishment, in the siege of the famous city of Maestricht. The city was defended by 8000 chosen men, and was fortified in every way that skill suggested.

The Prince of Orange was in command of the besiegers, and during the investment made great use of the Fifth and the other two English regiments with him.

These three regiments were formed in one brigade, and numbered 2600 men. They petitioned the Prince to assign a particular quarter to them and a separate command, so that they might have all the glory or bear all the shame of their achievements. They repeatedly distinguished themselves, beating back with great slaughter the sallies of the garrison. On July 30 a storming party of 200 men, furnished by the three regiments in equal proportions, attacked the Dauphin Bastion. They won a temporary triumph, at a cost in killed and wounded of 150 —75 per cent.,—but afterwards lost the ground they had gained.

A second attack on the bastion was made on August 4, when the storming party was formed of a detachment from the brigade, with another from the Dutch Foot Guards. The English attack was in the following order :—2 sergeants and 10 firelocks ; 1 sergeant and 12 grenadiers ;

1 officer, 1 sergeant, and 12 grenadiers; 1
lieutenant, 2 sergeants, and 30 firelocks; 1
sergeant and 12 men with half-pikes; 1 captain,
1 lieutenant, 2 sergeants, and 50 firelocks; 1
sergeant and 12 men with half-pikes; 1 captain,
1 lieutenant, 1 sergeant, and 28 men with spades
and shovels. The support—1 captain, 1 sergeant,
and 58 men.

The bastion was stormed with the utmost
determination. The English, gaining the lead
of the Dutch, first made a lodgment; but the
soldiers had hardly gained a footing when the
French sprang a mine and blew many of the
assailants into the air. Following this up with
a fierce attack, they retook the bastion—only
for a time. With renewed energy and fury
the English returned to the attack, and again
drove out the enemy and took the bastion.
The cost was heavy, half the officers and men
of the party being either killed or wounded.

Early on the morning of August 5 the
neglect of a sentry enabled 300 Swiss infantry
to sally from the city and surprise and capture
the English guard on the bastion; but a

reinforcement from the brigade dashed to the rescue of their comrades. With volleys of musketry and a shower of hand grenades they charged furiously upon and retook the bastion, drove out and chased the Swiss infantry, and pursued them so relentlessly that of the 300 all were destroyed except a score who regained the safety of the city

By way of showing his appreciation of this bravery and energy, the Prince of Orange gave each of the three regiments a fat ox and six sheep, which they killed and hung upon poles in sight of the army, to divide into equal parts to each company. "Some of the Dutch, murmuring at this bounty to the English in particular, were told that the same was given to save Dutchmen's lives, and therefore they ought to be thankful to His Highness for it."

This famous siege dragged on, the valour of the assailants being met by the resolute behaviour of the defenders. Everything was ready for a general assault when a French army of overwhelming numbers advanced to the city's relief. The Prince of Orange, seeing no chance of success, immediately raised the siege and retired. The three English regiments were sent into " quarters of refreshment " in Holland, having suffered very severe losses, and nearly half the surviving officers and men being wounded. At this time a misunderstanding occurred between Colonel (afterwards Sir John) Fenwick, of the Fifth, and the Prince, and the colonel resigned his commission. Though the siege had failed, yet Maestricht was restored to the Dutch in 1678. In 1748 it was besieged by the French, who gained possession, and in 1794 they again became masters of the city. Maestricht was in 1814 made part of the kingdom of the Netherlands.

In 1677—April 11—the Fifth took part in the battle of Mont Cassel, under the Prince of Orange. The English Brigade fought against great disadvantages of numbers and ground, and the Prince was forced to retreat with his artillery and baggage. Afterwards the Prince went to England, where, on November 14, he married the Princess Mary, the presumptive heiress of the Crown.

A year later—1678—the regiment was encamped near the ground where, in 1815, the battle of Waterloo was fought. It took part in the battle of Casthau, near Mons, where it sustained serious losses. Lieutenant-Colonel Archer and Lieutenant Charlton and about 50 men were killed, and Major Hales, Captains Charlton, Coleman, Floyd, and Dupuy ; Lieutenants Augerne, Marchany, and Wilson ; and Ensigns Barnwell and Arnesby were wounded, with more than 100 men. For four years the regiment—then known as Colonel Wisely's Regiment—was employed on garrison duty at Grave, remaining in the Dutch service with the other five British regiments, subject to a liability to return to England when they were wanted by the King. Under this treaty the six regiments were, in 1685, applied for by James II. to assist in putting down the rebellion in Scotland which was headed by the Duke of Argyle, and that in England which was led by the Duke of Monmouth. The services of the troops, however, were not needed, as by the time they landed in England the risings had been crushed.

The three English regiments — Colonel Thomas Monk's, now the Fifth; Colonel Sir Henry Bellasis', now the Royal Warwickshire Regiment, formerly the Sixth Foot; Colonel Alexander Cannon's, afterwards disbanded — were on the English establishment from June 5 to August 3, 1685. The six regiments returned to Holland, where they were employed in garrison duty. In 1687 James demanded the return of the British regiments in the Dutch service; but the States-General, in concert with the Prince of Orange, determined not to part with these favourite troops, especially as they expected to have urgent need of their services. No restraint, however, was placed upon the officers, who were allowed either to remain in Holland or to return to England, as they wished. Out of 240 officers only 60 embraced the latter alternative, the rest binding themselves "to stand by and defend the Prince of Orange against all persons whatsoever." Religious feeling ran high, and the Papal leanings of James II. found but feeble support amongst the British regiments in Holland.

One of the officers who left the Dutch service at this time was Captain John Bernardi of the Fifth, a soldier who had fought in many actions and received several wounds. He obtained a commission in the regiment on its formation in 1674. At the Revolution in 1688 he adhered to King James, and served in Ireland and Scotland in that monarch's cause. Subsequently he lived in London, and being implicated in the plot to assassinate King William in 1696, he was imprisoned. Although his guilt could not be established and he was never brought to trial, yet Bernardi was detained in prison by an Act of Parliament expressly passed for that purpose. After remaining in prison for more than thirty years Bernardi wrote his life, which was published in 1729. The book contains much that is of interest relating to the earlier years of the Fifth.

To this period also belonged Cornet George Carleton, another historian of the times. While the Fifth were in England Carleton left the Dutch service, and obtained a commission in a newly-raised regiment on the English establishment. He served as a volunteer with the Fleet under the Duke of York in 1672 and 1673, and in the same capacity with the army commanded by the Prince of Orange, from 1674 to 1676, when he obtained a commission in the Fifth. He saw much fighting, and his experiences have been preserved in his memoirs, which were highly successful as a book, and admittedly contain the best account extant of the services of the Earl of Peterborough in Spain.

When in 1688 many of the English nobility solicited the armed aid of the Prince of Orange in averting the threatened Papal domination of Great Britain, the Prince and the States-General permitted the six British regiments to return, and these troops sailed from Holland for their native land. The Prince's army consisted of about 15,000 men, of whom "the most formidable were the six British regiments." After some delay, arising from bad weather, the army put to sea on November 1, 1688, "the trumpets sounding, the haut-boys playing, the soldiers and seamen shouting, and a crowd of spectators on the shore breathing forth their wishes after them." The Fifth landed at Brixham Key, two miles from Dartmouth, and marched to Exeter ; later they marched to London. The threatened revolution did not come to pass. James fled to France, and William and Mary ascended the throne.

In 1689 the regiment was permanently placed on the English establishment, and taking date from June 5, 1685, the day on which it first received pay from the British Crown, it ranked as the Fifth Regiment of Foot in the British Line.

CHAPTER II

FIGHTS IN IRELAND

THE battle of the Boyne, the siege of Limerick, and operations against bands of armed Roman Catholic peasantry called Rapparees demanded the services of the Fifth for a couple of years after their return from Holland. Ireland had become the seat of war, and in that country James was at the head of the Roman Catholics and a French auxiliary force. The Duke of Schomberg commanded the Protestants and English troops.

The Fifth were ordered to Ireland in 1690. Embarking at Bristol, they landed at Belfast, and in June pitched their tents in the neighbourhood of Armagh, where four regiments of English infantry, with three regiments of Danish horse and eight of foot, were encamped.

King William having landed in Ireland, the Fifth marched to Dundalk, where the army was assembled, and on July 1 the enemy were attacked in their position on the banks of the Boyne. In this engagement King William inflicted a severe defeat on his father-in-law, who, out of 30,000 troops, lost 1500. The Protestant army, out of the same number, lost about 500. James fled to Dublin, thence to Waterford, and escaped to France. Schomberg was killed in the battle. He was shot by mistake by the soldiers of his own regiment as he was crossing the Boyne.

In April 1691 the regiment was quartered at Mountmellick, and, like the rest of the troops, suffered from the raids of the Rapparees. Those bands remained in hiding during the day, and prowled about at night, committing every sort of depredation. To check these outrages a detachment was sent of 200 men of the Fifth, commanded by Major Rider, with 100 men of Lord George Hamilton's Regiment, and 50 troopers of Colonel Byerley's Horse, now the 6th Dragoon Guards. The whole force was under Major Wood,—afterwards celebrated as General Wood,—and marched from Mountmellick on the night of May 4.

Divided into small parties, they made their way for several miles through the woods and bogs, encountering lurking bands of the enemy. They killed 70 men and captured a number of cattle, which Wood sent to Mountmellick under a guard of 30 men. Next morning Wood, with 34 horsemen and 30 foot, engaged 400 of the enemy's regular forces not far from Castle Cuff. This little band was reinforced by a detachment of 80 men of the Fifth, and with his 34 horsemen and 110 foot Wood boldly attacked the enemy's column. While the troopers trampled upon and cut down the enemy, the foot slung their muskets and drew their swords and pursued the enemy for a considerable distance. The Irish had 150 killed on the spot, and 127 of their number were taken prisoners—a total loss of 277 ; whereas the loss of Wood's force was only one corporal killed, one adjutant, two foot soldiers, and one trooper wounded. On the 12th of the same month another party of the regiment, when scouring the woods, killed 18 Rapparees and took several prisoners. In June the Fifth took part in the siege of Athlone, which began on the 19th. On the 30th the grenadier company was included in the storming party.

The attack was made at 6 P.M., when the forlorn hope, consisting of Captain Sandys, with 2 lieutenants and 60 grenadiers, all in armour, entered the Shannon, which was breast high. They were followed by the rest of the storming party, some of whom passed by means of a bridge of boats, and the rest over planks placed across the broken arches of the stone bridge. In less than half an hour the town was taken, with a loss to the assailants of 12 men killed and 5 officers and 30 men wounded, the enemy's loss being about 500 killed.

The Fifth were actively employed in the siege of Limerick until that place surrendered on October 3. This conquest ended the war in Ireland, and the Fifth proceeded to England, landing near Chester on December 29.

Two months only passed before the Fifth embarked for Flanders to join the Allies in operations against the French ; but the regiment had scarcely landed when it was recalled to England to help to repel a threatened invasion by the French. The defeat of the French fleet near La Hogue by the combined English and Dutch fleets under Admirals Russell and Rooke prevented the descent, and the Fifth had a short spell of inactivity.

In 1693 the regiment took part in an expedition to Martinico, laying waste, with the rest of the forces, several French settlements in that island. The summer having been employed in this way, the Fifth returned to England in the autumn. By the end of the year they were back in Flanders, being one of the regiments chosen to reinforce the Allies after the heavy losses at the battle of Landen.

Again the regiment was commanded by King William, under whom it shared in the siege of Namur, forming part of the covering army. From Namur, which capitulated on August 22, the regiment marched to Nieuport, and encamped on the sand-hills near that town. The Fifth remained in the field until late in the season, when, as the weather was very cold and wet, they were ordered to build straw huts. Towards the end of October they marched to Bruges, and with that city they were closely associated until the end of the war. Before returning to England the regiment again encamped near Waterloo. In December 1697 the Fifth landed in England, and in the year following embarked for Ireland, where they were stationed during the early part of the war of the Spanish Succession.

In 1707 the Fifth were selected, with other three regiments, for service in Portugal. But operations in that country were flagging, and it was not until 1709 that the regiment was again called upon to exercise those fighting powers for which it was already famed.

The French and Spaniards having, on May 7, 1709, marched towards Campo Mayor, the Portuguese generals, against the advice of the Earl of Galway, determined to pass the Caya and attack the enemy. A great show was made by the Portuguese cavalry and artillery, who, having taken the lead, passed the river, gained the opposite heights, and opened a smart cannonade. When, however, the enemy advanced to charge, the cavalry and gunners faced about and galloped from the field, leaving their cannon behind. At this critical stage of the action the British Division, now consisting of seven regiments—fresh troops having arrived from home—came up and repulsed the enemy. The leading brigade of three regiments, commanded by Brigadier-General Pearce, recaptured the abandoned guns, but pressing too far, they were surrounded and made prisoners. Encouraged by this great success, the enemy made a desperate attack upon the Fifth, the 20th, the 39th, and Lord Paston's Regiments. These troops, though deserted by the whole of the cavalry, withstood the assaults, and enabled the Portuguese infantry to retire. They then, in the steadiest manner, effected their own retreat, occasionally halting and firing into their pursuers, of whom they destroyed 1000. The loss of the four regiments was only 150 killed and wounded. The Fifth acquired great honour on this occasion, which was a fit precursor to the brilliant feats that distinguished the regiment in the same country a hundred years later.

On October 5, 1710, the Fifth, 20th, and 39th Regiments stormed Xeres de los Cabaleros, on the river Ardilla, in Spanish Estremadura. The garrison surrendered a few minutes after the assault began, so that the assailants scored an easy victory.

The year 1711 was notable chiefly for the discovery of a clandestine treaty between the Crown of Portugal and the enemy, in which the Portuguese agreed to separate from the Allies. As an excuse for this extraordinary treatment of troops to whom they owed so much, "a mock battle was to have been fought, in which the British troops were to have been sacrificed." This treaty was broken off, and soon afterwards the British Government entered into negotiations with France.

From Portugal, the Fifth, in 1713, went to Gibraltar, where they remained in garrison for fifteen years. The protection of the fortress was given to the Fifth and their comrades, the 13th and 20th Regiments, now the Somersetshire Light Infantry, and the Lancashire Fusiliers. The establishment of the Fifth was 500, and while at Gibraltar they became as celebrated for good conduct and discipline as they had been on the field of battle for courage and devotion.

The Fifth, in 1727, shared in the defence of Gibraltar against a Spanish force of 20,000. The Spaniards encamped before the place in January, and spent many weeks in collecting their artillery, mortars, and stores. Troops were brought from all parts of the country, and the heavy guns from Cadiz and other fortified towns, so that nothing should be wanting which should help in the reduction of the Rock. These preparations were made before a declaration of war, and despite the protests of the Governor of Gibraltar. At a council of war, the officers commanding the regiments at Gibraltar resolved to make a determined opposition to the enemy, and on February 21 the garrison opened fire on the besiegers. The hostilities lasted for four months, the cannon roaring and the small arms crackling almost incessantly during the daytime,

and partially continuing throughout the night.
The Spaniards lost about 3000 men, burst many
of their guns, and made others useless, and at
the end of it all had to withdraw in defeat and
confusion. The garrison sustained a loss of
only 300. In addition, they suffered heavily
in their ordnance, which for the most part was
old and practically worthless. No fewer than
70 cannon and 30 mortars burst during the
siege.

In 1728 the Fifth left Gibraltar for Ireland,
where seven years were spent. Two years were
then passed in England, the regiment returning
to Ireland in 1737, and remaining in that country
for seventeen years. In 1752 the command of
the regiment was given to Colonel Whitefoord,
an officer who demands more than passing
mention, not only because of his personal
character, but because he was at the head of the
Fifth at a singularly interesting period of their
history. Colonel Whitefoord had been of great
service to the Government during the rebellion
in Scotland in 1745, and as a reward he was
appointed lieutenant-colonel of the Fifth in

September 1751. The regiment was at that
time commanded by General Irwin, and in
accordance with the custom of the day was
known as Irwin's Regiment. In November 1752
Whitefoord was given the colonelcy in succession
to Irwin, but he died after holding the office
for a brief period. Whitefoord first entered
the sea service in 1718, but he joined the Army
two years later, apparently serving in the ranks
of a cavalry regiment. It was not long before
he got a commission, and ultimately reached the
post he held at the time of his death, which took
place at Galway, where the Fifth were stationed,
on January 2, 1753.

Whitefoord died like a brave officer and an
unassuming English gentleman. He expressly
made known, in writing, this, his last wish :—
" Lieutenant-Colonel Charles Whitefoord begs
ye favour of Captain Dering that he will take
ye direction of his funeral, who desires to be
buried out of consecrated ground, without any
stone or decoration on his grave, and without
military honours. But begs that Captain Dering
will inform ye garrison, that such as pleases

will meet where he appoints, and drink a hearty glass to his jorney."

A century and a half ago it was a profitable thing to be the colonel of a regiment. Before numbers were instituted, regiments were known by their colonels' names, and on the colonel a vast responsibility rested ; in fact there was between the Crown and him a sort of contract by which the regiment was recruited, paid, and maintained. The colonel, through the regimental agent, received the pay and allowances for the establishment, and made his own terms as to recruiting, through his captains. This allowance, which covered clothing, went to what was known as the " stock purse " of the regiment, and after the accounts of the year had been settled, the balance became the captains', amongst whom it was divided. Accordingly, the officers had a pecuniary interest in maintaining the regiment and preventing desertion and waste, so that it is obvious that false returns and fraud were frequent occurrences. It happened, too, that when men were badly wanted, and this was often the case, no means were too contemptible to fill the ranks.

An Act was in 1779 actually passed for impressing soldiers, with the result that " thieves, too lame to run and too poor to bribe, were caught." But (adds Grose) " the soldiers considered it a grievous and cruel insult to have these men forced on them, and loudly complained to their officers." " Fraud on the Government and harsh treatment of the soldiers were," the authors of *The Army Book for the British Empire* state, " for long, characteristics of our army institution."

This explanation has been needful to make clear the following quaint letter which Colonel Whitefoord wrote in 1752 to an officer :—

" I have the pleasure of yours, with one from Lieutenant M'Laughlin, which gives me a good deal of concern. He says men are very hard to get, and has sent over but six, whereof two have been in the service. I have fatally experienced the bad consequence of giving the recruiting officers a latitude, and must have a very good opinion of the man to whom I give a discretionary power. To change low men for others no taller is folly, and not to be compleat in Aprile is dangerous : therefor lads under 18 of 5 ft. 7 in. I consent to take, but would alter the instructions no further. Now I must reveal my secret in order to make you easie and procure the general's approbation, whose will shall always be to me a law. Our drummers are sightly fellows. I propose turning as many of them into the ranks as will compleat us, and listing boys in their roome. That saves us with the commissary, and does not exhaust the exchequer. After the review I discharge the boys, and then shall have a fine sum in the stock purse. At the same time the general saves the cloathing. When winter comes we will send a greater number of officers, by which method we shall save to the general, put money in the captain's pocket, and effectuat our scheme of not haveing (at least) the worst regiment in Ireland. I have a plot of making our sergeants fine at a small expence. You see their cloaths are new lapell'd. That I shall propose to alter, and have them looped up like the men's with a half silver lace, which you must buy in England. By this means we shall make a show with economy. For the cloath saved will near purchase the lace, and as I have communicated this to nobody, I hope you will keep it to yourself."

The letter is not only most interesting in itself, but is also of great value as affording a glimpse into the inner life of the Fifth a century and a half ago ; indeed there is much in the Whitefoord Papers generally which is of peculiar value regimentally.

CHAPTER III

THE CAP AND THE COLOUR

FOR thirty years, during most of which they were quartered in Ireland, the Fifth had enjoyed peace ; when in 1758 another war broke out, the regiment formed part of an expedition to reduce the French naval power and make a diversion in favour of the Hanoverians. On May 25 the regiment embarked at Cowes, 888 men strong, and its grenadier company were the first to land on the French coast. This was on the evening of June 5, when seven companies of French foot and three troops of dragoons were met and speedily dispersed. The army on the 7th advanced in two columns, and the Fifth encamped in the evening about a mile from St. Maloes. After sunset they furnished a detachment which, with detachments from the other regiments, fired the magazines and shipping, and having destroyed a valuable fleet and all the stores, re-embarked for England. This expedition may rank as one of the shortest and most successful of its kind. In the following August the Fifth took part in a second expedition to the coast of France. Cherbourg was captured, and the harbour, forts, ordnance, and magazines destroyed. Iron cannon to the number of 173 and 3 mortars were thus made useless, while 22 fine brass guns and 2 brass mortars were brought to England. These trophies were inspected by George II. in Hyde Park on September 16, and were afterwards taken in procession to the Tower. In September a third successful descent on the French coast— Brittany—was shared in by the Fifth, who on these occasions lost 95 men. Three triumphant undertakings of such a character make the year 1758 one of considerable interest in the annals of the Fifth.

The war in Hanover and the neighbouring States continuing, the Fifth, in 1760, were ordered to Germany, where the grenadier company, with the grenadier companies of the other regiments, composed two battalions which, united with the Scots Brigade, usually formed the advanced guard of the army. This campaign added greatly to the renown of the Fifth, the regiment itself and the detached grenadiers displaying the utmost courage and endurance from first to last. Landing near Bremen, the Fifth, on July 10, had a sharp skirmish with the French on the heights of Corbach. Late at night on the 30th the Fifth, with the rest of the troops, marched to attack the enemy in his position on the heights of Warbourg. The attack was delivered early on the following morning. The grenadier company of the Fifth was in the column which began the attack, and highly distinguished itself. The brunt of the action fell on the British grenadiers and the German corps who began the action, for the French withdrew before the English infantry arrived. In his despatch concerning this affair the Marquis of Granby said, " No troops could show more eagerness than they showed. Many of the men, from the heat of the weather, and overstraining themselves to get on through morasses and difficult ground, suddenly dropped down on their march." The grenadier company on September 5 gallantly and successfully surprised a French force in the town of Zierenberg, and afterwards was engaged in an attempt to surprise the enemy's camp at Rheinberg on the morning of October 16, when a sharp action was fought at the convent of Campen. In February 1761 the regiment forced its way through deep snow into Hesse-Cassel, where it achieved success in several conflicts with the enemy. In March it returned to its former quarters, but was again in the field in June.

While encamped in front of Kirch-Denkern the Fifth and other British troops were attacked on July 15, but drove the enemy back. The attack was renewed next morning with great determination, but again it failed. The Fifth were very prominent in this engagement. After five hours' fighting some disorder was observed in the ranks of the enemy. Instantly the Fifth took advantage of the situation, and charged and routed the foe. At the same time the grenadier battalion, of which the grenadier company of the Fifth formed a part, made prisoners the Regiment of Rouge (formerly Belsunce) with its colours and cannon. The Fifth suffered considerable loss in this action. After being engaged in several minor affairs—including a skirmish on November 10, in which the grenadier company fought knee-deep in snow—the winter was passed "among the rude peasantry of Osnaburg."

All these affairs were but the sharpening of the Fifth for that triumph at Wilhelmstahl which has conferred lasting glory on the regiment and British troops. On June 4 a battle was fought at Groebenstein and in the woods of Wilhelmstahl. The enemy having taken post at Groebenstein, Prince Ferdinand of Brunswick determined to surprise them in their camp. Accordingly the army was formed into several columns. The Fifth, who were part of the centre column, left their camp before daylight on the morning of June 24, and at four o'clock crossed the Dymel at Liebenau. After advancing nine miles through a rugged and woody country, they arrived before the enemy's camp and opened a sharp fire. "Surprised and confounded," the French abandoned their camp, leaving their tents standing, and began their retreat. Instantly a French division was thrown into the woods of Wilhelmstahl to favour this movement, and against that division the right and centre columns of the Allies advanced.

The Fifth, taking the lead of the attacking column, threw themselves into the wood and opened fire upon the French with destructive effect. At the same time the enemy's rear was attacked. A stubborn resistance was made, but the Fifth pressed irresistibly forward, and admirably paved the way for the troops which followed. In spite of the fact that the British were opposed to the flower of the French infantry, the enemy was badly beaten. Except two battalions which got away, the whole French force surrendered to the Fifth, the total number of prisoners being 2732, of whom 162 were officers.

After the surrender, an officer of the Fifth, who went up to receive the enemy's colours from their standard-bearer, was shot dead by a French sergeant, who was standing near. The sergeant was instantly put to death, and the colours were quietly taken possession of by the victorious Fifth.

In this brilliant and exceptional affair the loss of the Fifth was very slight. Prince Ferdinand was so much impressed by the extraordinary valour of the regiment on this occasion that he presented a snuff-box to the commanding officer, Colonel Marley, and this relic is still treasured by the officers to-day. But the honouring of the Fifth for that action did not stop there; the men were allowed to exchange their hats for the French grenadier caps, and for many years afterwards the regiment wore a fusilier's cap instead of the hat then used by the infantry of the line. Furthermore, a third colour was carried by the regiment in memory of the victory. This colour was retained until 1836, when in place of it "Wilhelmstahl" was authorised to be borne on the colours and appointments. "Wilhelmstahl" is the first, as it is the most unique, of the battle honours of the Fifth.

In reference to this action the *London Gazette* said :—" Prince Ferdinand pursued and pressed upon them as close as possible, and they would without doubt have been entirely routed if Monsieur de Stainville had not thrown himself, with the Grenadiers of France, the Royal Grenadiers, the Regiment of Aquitaine, and other corps, being the flower of the French infantry, into the woods of Wilhelmstahl to cover their retreat. That resolution cost him dear, his whole infantry having been taken, killed, or dispersed, after a very gallant defence, excepting two battalions which found means to get off. Some of these troops had before surrendered to Lord Granby's corps, and upon the coming up of the army, the remainder, after one fire, surrendered to the Fifth Regiment of Foot."

In 1763 the Fifth marched from Germany through Holland to Williamstadt, where they embarked for England, landing early in March. By the beginning of June they were again quartered in Ireland, where the next ten years were passed. During this period the Fifth were so remarkable for their cleanliness and attention to dress and appointments that the men were usually called " The Shiners." While in Ireland —early in 1767—the Order of Merit was established. This was a system of honorary distinctions for long-continued good behaviour which had the most beneficial effect on the regiment, smart and efficient though it was; and the result was the possession by the Fifth of a body of non-commissioned officers the like of which few regiments could claim. These medals were of three classes, and given only to soldiers who for seven, fourteen, or twenty-one years had never incurred the censure of a court-martial. The decorations were conferred at the head of the assembled battalion by the commanding officer, and if—rare event—the possessor of this valued distinction forfeited his recommendation to continue to hold it, the medal was cut from his breast by the drum-major as publicly as he had been invested with it. The first, or lowest class of medal, was of gilt metal, with the regimental badge of St. George and the Dragon on one side, and the motto, *Quo fata vocant*, and on the reverse

"Vth Foot, Merit." The second was of silver, with the badge and motto on one side, and on the other, "Reward of fourteen years' military merit"; while the third was similar, but was inscribed with the recipient's name, "A. B., for twenty-one years' good and faithful service as a soldier, had received from his commanding officers this honourable testimony of his merit." Those who received the third medal also got an oval badge of the colour of the facings of the regiment. This badge, which was worn on the right breast, was embroidered round with gold and silver wreaths, the word "Merit" being inscribed in letters of gold in the centre. For nearly a century this treasured distinction was enjoyed by the Fifth. It was finally abolished by a letter dated February 23, 1856.

CHAPTER IV

THE WINNING OF THE PLUME

WHILE in Ireland the Fifth were frequently engaged in the Revenue service, and from time to time were called upon to suppress bands of armed peasants known by such titles as Whiteboys, Hearts of Steel, and Hearts of Oak.

When in 1774 the deplorable events between Great Britain and her North American colonies necessitated the sending of additional troops across the Atlantic, the Fifth were chosen to proceed on that service. The regiment was part of the force which caused the first blood to be shed in this memorable war. This was at Lexington, not far from Boston, on April 18, 1775. This skirmish was followed by an extraordinary march of about thirty-five miles, on a hot day, to Charlestown, from which place the troops were ferried across the river to Boston under cover of the fire of the men-of-war. The whole province being now in arms, an immense number of men invested Boston on the land side, and on the morning of June 17 it was found that they had constructed works on high ground beyond the river, known as Bunker's Hill.

The Fifth formed part of a force which was ordered to attack the heights, and the force managed to land without opposition and form up on some high ground near the shore. It was clear that the enemy was determined to defend his post, and under cover of the fire of the ships of war the troops went bravely to the assault. It required high courage, too, to face a defence like that on such a day, for the heat was great and the hill that was stormed was steep. The men were encumbered with three days' provisions; they had their knapsacks on their backs, and altogether carried a weight of 125 lbs. They had to force their way through grass which reached to their knees, and was intersected with walls and fences of various enclosures. Further, they were met by a fierce and well-directed fire, so that the conquest of Bunker's Hill became an unusually severe task. Twice the British troops were stopped in their assault, and twice they returned to the charge. Nothing but sheer pluck and physical power could have ensured success, and it speaks well for the quality of the Fifth in those days that they gained their goal despite almost overwhelming obstacles. They made a last grand rush with fixed bayonets, and having actually come face to face with the foe, they drove him out of the works and remained masters of the situation Well might General Burgoyne say of Bunker's Hill that "the Fifth has behaved the best and suffered the most," for in the assault the regiment had a loss of officers and men which proved a very serious drain on its resources.

This success was great, but the army remained at Boston in a state of blockade, and so hard pressed for fresh provisions and other necessaries were the troops, that live cattle and vegetables, and even fuel, were dispatched from

England. Many of the ships containing these supplies, however, were either wrecked or fell into the hands of the Americans, and the consequence was that sickness and death made havoc amongst the imprisoned soldiers. Side by side with this scarcity of food was the renewed activity of the enemy, who suffered from no such lack of needful things. Evacuation became inevitable, and in March 1776 the army embarked from Boston and went to Halifax ; but most of the troops had to remain on board ship, as the town had neither accommodation nor food enough for them.

For several months the Fifth were engaged in minor operations in various districts, at all times mindful of their reputation, and enduring privations and lean living with a fortitude that earned for them unstinted admiration. Between the fight at Bunker's Hill and another severe action in which the Fifth greatly distinguished themselves, they were concerned in the attack on Long Island (August 27, 1776), the capture of White Plains (October 28) and Fort Washington (November 16). In 1777 they were quartered in the Island of New Jersey, and on October 4 took part in the defence of Germantown, where they fought bravely and suffered severely. The next year, 1778, was an eventful one, for during it the Fifth earned the right to the plume which for so long a period has been peculiar to the regiment. In September 300 men of the regiment and New Jersey Volunteers embarked in transports on an expedition to Little Egg Harbour, in New Jersey, a place which in those days was noted for its connection with privateers. On reaching the harbour the detachment went on board small vessels, which, with several row-galleys, proceeded twenty miles up the river to Chestnut Neck, where, under the cover of the galley's fire, the troops landed. Of that little expedition the Fifth made a thoroughly good bit of work, for having routed the enemy's forces which opposed the descent, they chased it into the woods, and then returned and destroyed the village, as well as several store-houses and armed vessels. Subsequently a night excursion was made ten miles farther up the river, the result being that the troops surprised some companies of the enemy in their quarters, put many to death at the point of the bayonet, and destroyed the enemy's shelter. This was accomplished with the loss of only two killed and two wounded of the Fifth.

As soon as this detachment had returned, the regiment was ordered to form part of an expedition against the French West Indies, and sailed from Sandy Hook on November 3, under the command of Lieutenant-Colonel (afterwards Sir William) Medows, its chief. The expedition reached St. Lucie on December 13, and immediately the Fifth, by another exhibition of valour, secured a distinction as unique as that of the third colour. This work began with the capture of the town of Morne Fortuné on December 14. The Fifth, having seized the town, the governor's house, and the hospital and barracks, occupied an important post named La Vigie, situated on a tongue of land commanding the north side of the Carenage Harbour, and separated by that harbour from the rest of the army. Meanwhile the French fleet had arrived off the harbour and had disembarked 9000 men, and on the 18th this force attacked the handful of soldiers of the Fifth under Medows. The enemy, in three columns, made three fierce attacks, and were beaten off each time. They lost about 400 killed and 1100 wounded, while the British killed numbered only 10, and the wounded 130.

Once more the English had overpowered the French, and the conduct of the Fifth was signalised by the granting to them of the right to wear a white plume in the cap instead of the red and white tuft worn by other regiments of the line, the Fifth having taken from the bodies of slain French Grenadiers enough white feathers to decorate every man in the regiment. Those were the days in which colours were essentially a rallying-point, and Medows, who was in command, at one great crisis of the battle, finding that his ammunition was nearly done, drew up his gallant band in front of them, and waving his sword, exclaimed, "Soldiers, as long as you have a bayonet to point against an enemy's breast, defend these colours!" Besides uttering these inspiring words he set a glorious personal example, for he refused to quit his post, though wounded severely in the right arm, and continued to ride from point to point until the attack was over and the victory assured. In a letter from Morne Fortuné, dated December 19, General Grant said: "I cannot express how much I feel obliged to you, and the troops under your command, for repulsing, with so much spirit and bravery, so great a body of the enemy, and own it was just what I expected from you and them."

From this time until the end of the century the Fifth served on both sides of the Atlantic, renewing their associations with Ireland. In 1784 they received the denomination of the Northumberland Regiment, in compliment to Earl Percy, who for sixteen years had held the command, and was then promoted to the colonelcy of the second troop of Horse Grenadier Guards.

The colours of the Fifth, which time and

battle had reduced to shreds, were in 1785 replaced by a new set. This was on St. George's Day, on the evening of which "the men dined sumptuously in the barrack-yard by companies, at the expense of their lately promoted colonel, Earl Percy."

Just before the century ended, the Fifth were once more in Holland, the country in which so many of their fighting years had been passed, and where they did good service in spite of hardships which the Duke of York in General Orders described as "insupportable." The Fifth were amongst the last of the British troops to leave Holland in 1799. The regiment had been divided into two battalions of 800 each this year, and these battalions, after a short stay in England, were ordered to Gibraltar in 1800.

CHAPTER V

THE opening years of the nineteenth century were uneventful for the Fifth, but the critical and disturbed state of politics made it impossible for the regiment to remain long inactive. In 1805 the 1st Battalion embarked for the defence of Hanover, but the *Helder* transport, containing the left wing of the battalion, was wrecked off the Helder—strange coincidence—and the officers and men were made prisoners by the Dutch. The *Helder* was a large armed transport, formerly a Dutch brig-of-war. She was taken at the Helder in 1799. The troops on board were commanded by Major Henry King, Fifth Regiment, afterwards General Sir Henry King, who served many years in the Fifth, and commanded the regiment during the

Peninsular War. This officer left amongst his papers a most interesting MS. diary, inscribed on the title page:—"Henry King, Major, 5th Regiment, Enkhurgsen, North Holland, January 10th, 1806, Prisoner on Parole, 'Spero Meliora.'"

It was feared that these prisoners of the Fifth, numbering about 250, would be marched into the interior of France; but they were unexpectedly released and sent home. In his manuscript diary, "Account of the Return to Regimental Head Quarters, Fifth Regiment, at Rye, of the Three Companies of the Regiment who were taken Prisoners of War in Holland in 1805," Lieutenant (subsequently Lieutenant-General) Nicholas Hamilton, K.H., Fifth Foot, said the men were pitiable objects. They were almost naked, and their appearance gave proof enough of what they had suffered from poor and scanty food and the damp and filth of the prison ships on board of which they were confined. But crippled and ragged as some of them were, they speedily forgot their sufferings, "as they each received sufficient money to drown all their cares in good beer on their arrival in quarters."

The right wing, on returning to England in 1806, was in September joined by the left wing, which had been liberated by an exchange of prisoners. In that year also the 1st Battalion sailed in the expedition to South America, and in addition to suffering much discomfort and enduring many privations, took part in the attack on Buenos Ayres on July 5. The Fifth had their post towards the convent of Recolata, and in the plan for the general attack were formed in two divisions, with orders to penetrate the streets immediately in front. Early in the morning the troops advanced through what appeared to be deserted streets, but suddenly, at a given signal, the whole of the male population appeared, and from the windows and flat roofs of the houses, which were crowded with armed men, there came a furious and destructive fire. It was also found that the streets were crossed by ditches and protected by guns, and that an advance, if not actually impossible, was very difficult. The task was one for the bayonet only, for orders had been given that not a shot was to be fired until the great square was reached. The Fifth, with fixed bayonets, forced a way through the streets as far as the river and seized the church and convent of St. Catalina. Thence they moved to the Plaza de Toros, where the British force captured a large number of guns, a vast quantity of ammunition, and many prisoners. But three British regiments had been forced to surrender, as it was impossible for them to make effective answer to the fire which was poured upon them. Altogether the assailants in this contest lost 2500 men, the Fifth having a heavy list of casualties. On the following day Lieutenant-General Whitelocke, commanding the British force, agreed to vacate Buenos Ayres, and the army returned to England after a long voyage, marked by much suffering from shortness of water and provisions. On his return Whitelocke was brought to trial, the Government being forced by the country to take that step. In January 1809 he was court-martialed and dismissed the service.

The drummers of the Fifth were in 1807

clothed in white, with white and red lace, instead of gosling green.

In the summer of 1808 the Fifth began that long connection with the Peninsula which was to make so serious a drain on their resources, but which was also to give the regiment many of its greatest honours. On August 9 the 1st Battalion landed in Portugal, and immediately joined the army of Sir Arthur Wellesley. Within a few days it had earned for the regiment the first of the Peninsular distinctions, " Roleia," and had enabled the Fifth to claim the honour of being amongst the first of the British troops to come in contact with the enemy.

The village of Roleia crowns an eminence, which again is flanked by a range of hills on the one hand, and by rugged mountains on the other. Immediately in front of it at that time was a sandy plain, not woody, but studded with firs and shrubs, and in its rear were four or five passes, leading through the mountains. In this strong situation the French awaited the approach of the British army. But when Roleia had been reached it was found that the peculiarly difficult nature of the ground and the extremely narrow openings allowed of no more than five British battalions, a few companies of British light infantry; and a brigade of Portuguese being brought into action. The Portuguese infantry moved on the right, through the pass next that, upon the right, through which the light companies of Hill's Brigade, supported by the Fifth, were ordered to penetrate. The forcing of the third pass was entrusted to the 9th and 29th Regiments, the fourth to the 45th, and the fifth to the 82nd. Of his immense natural advantages the enemy made the utmost, and contested every inch of ground with the greatest confidence and stubbornness. Defeated in the end, he yet managed to make good his retreat, with the loss of 3 guns and about 1000 men. But for an order to halt which was given by a British general, the French could have been pursued and destroyed; as it was, they were able to rally and retreat in admirable order.

Wellesley in his despatch said, "I cannot sufficiently applaud the conduct of the troops throughout this action. The enemy's positions were formidable, and he took them up with his usual ability and celerity, and defended them most gallantly. I must observe that, although we had such a superiority of numbers employed in the operations of this day, the troops actually engaged in the heat of the action were, from unavoidable circumstances, only the Fifth, Ninth, Twenty-ninth, the riflemen of the Sixtieth and Ninety-fifth, and the flank companies of Major-General Hill's Brigade, being in number by no means equal to that of the enemy ; their conduct therefore deserves the highest commendation."

Four days later the Fifth gained their next Peninsular honour—"Vimiera." In this severe struggle, August 21, the 1st Battalion of the regiment formed, with the 9th and 38th Regiments, the first brigade, and were posted on the mountain on the right of the village. Vimiera, standing in the midst of a beautiful valley two or three miles from the sea, offered every requisite for a desperate contest, and enabled the French to make preparations, unseen, for an attack which would have taken a less watchful man than

Wellesley by surprise. The French advanced like troops who were used to victory and resolved to win, and only after a most valiant effort to defeat the British were they themselves routed at all points with exceptional slaughter. Of 12,000 or 13,000 men whom they brought into the field, between 3000 and 4000 fell, besides many prisoners. The total British loss was 783 killed, wounded, and missing.

From Portugal the 1st Battalion of the Fifth marched into Spain to help the people of that country in their resistance to the French. But when, after rapidly traversing 400 miles, the little British army found that their allies had been routed and dispersed, there began that terrible retreat to Corunna which ended with the glorious action of the 16th of January 1809, and gave to the Fifth the right to have "Corunna" emblazoned on their colours. In that forced retreat of 250 miles under Moore, the Fifth, owing to their appalling privations and meetings with the enemy, sustained a loss which has never been correctly known; but when the 1st Battalion was mustered on its return to England in February 1809, it was found that 132 men were missing. In the battle of Corunna the officer commanding the Fifth distinguished himself greatly. One horse being shot under him, he mounted another, and was at length shot dead. The command of the battalion then devolved upon Major Emes, who for this service received a medal.

Roleia, Vimiera, and Corunna had enabled the Fifth to share largely in the honourable but disastrous first British campaign in the Peninsula.

Only sufficient time passed on returning to England to allow the battalion to be fully equipped and completed to more than a thousand rank and file when it was ordered to join the expedition to Walcheren, that splendidly equipped large force from which so much was hoped. The expedition proved abortive and disastrous, and of the subsequent terrible loss from disease the Fifth suffered their proportion. The swamp fever attacked 600 of the men, and on the Island of Walcheren itself, and later in England, carried off large numbers. The Walcheren Expedition claims a separate chapter, but before dealing with that deplorable undertaking, the record of the regiment may be carried to a point from which the narrative may treat of the resumed campaign in the Peninsula.

The Fifth were represented at Talavera, July 27 and 28, 1809, by a detachment of the 1st Battalion, which had been left in Portugal when the battalion advanced into Spain. This detachment had been added to a battalion of detachments under Lieutenant-Colonel Copson of the Fifth, who received a medal for Talavera. The detachment in September reinforced the 2nd Battalion, which had proceeded to Portugal from Ireland. The 2nd Battalion took part in the battles of Busaco (September 27, 1810), Fuentes d'Onor (May 5, 1811), and the second siege of Badajoz, and was afterwards employed in the blockade of Ciudad Rodrigo.

CHAPTER VI

A DISASTROUS EXPEDITION

WHEN the regiment embarked for Walcheren it was in every way fit for the severest service. In his diary of the Walcheren Expedition and siege of Flushing, Lieutenant-General Nicholas Hamilton said, " Though we had so very lately returned from the campaign in Spain, I never witnessed the Regiment in such health and high discipline. . . . Indeed its appearance was the astonishment of the whole army." July though it was when the Fifth began their preparations for embarkation, yet the weather was so bad that it might have been winter ; but " booths were put up, and liquors of all descriptions consoled the soldiers for the inconveniences of wet weather."

The Fifth embarked on H.M.S. *Bellona*, and

while waiting with the rest of the warships and transports for a fair wind had the constant mortification of seeing seven Russian line-of-battle ships which were included in the Convention of Cintra, "and which by right should have been the just reward of the bravery displayed by our troops at the battles of Roleia and Vimiera in Portugal." On making an unopposed landing on Sunday, July 30, three days' cooked provisions were served out to the troops.

The disembarkation was made in a heavy rain, and the men had to wade up to the middle before they landed. On August 1 the British came in contact with the enemy, and had many casualties, the Fifth acquitting themselves in a manner worthy of a regiment fresh from the Peninsula. On the 2nd a man of the Fifth received a very strange wound. "The ball was extracted from his skull, cut in different shapes." It was generally remarked that the prisoners who were taken were always drunk, as they received an extraordinary allowance of spirits when sent on outposts, and that the enemy's fire was always more brisk after the hour at which they were supposed to have received this "gratuity." By August 3 the casualties of the Fifth were 5 killed and 40 wounded. Many of the latter died of their injuries. The weather continued miserably bad —the men were wet even in their huts, but so far they continued in good health and spirits.

The garrison of Flushing made a sortie on August 7 with the object of destroying the British batteries, now almost ready to open fire. The post defended by Hamilton was fiercely attacked, but the Fifth drove the enemy back, his dead lying in heaps across the road. Hamilton was shot through the thigh, so severely that after a month's " most excruciating torture" amputation was necessary. By the time the enemy withdrew that day the Fifth had lost between 60 and 70 killed and wounded, the flank companies of the regiment being the heaviest sufferers.

The General Orders of the day were most flattering to the Fifth, and the prisoners taken from the 48th Regiment of French Infantry, the force opposed to the Fifth, declared that they had never seen anything to equal the firmness of our troops. Some officers of the 48th asserted that their regiment alone could not have lost less than 500 men. Major Bird, of the Fifth, with a few men of his company, was taken prisoner, having become separated from the regiment and surrounded. Ensign Walton's life was saved by his greatcoat, which, rolled up and slung on his back, expended the force of a bullet which penetrated to the skin. Hamilton was removed to a neighbouring village, his sufferings being greatly increased by the sorrow of his father, who closely attended him, and the grief of his brother William. The subsequent portions of the diary were based largely on what the writer heard, but they bear the impress of reliability.

The weather continued very unfavourable, the troops being exposed night and day to the constant rain, protected only by huts made of branches of trees, and lying upon beds of straw which were spread upon the oozing, swampy ground. The work in the trenches, too, was done while the men were ankle-deep in mud and water. Yet so long as the troops were actively employed in the siege no particular sickness prevailed. It was only when Flushing was in their possession, and mind and body were less actively engaged, that sickness made its fearful ravages. "The new turned-up soil, soaked with rain, was the only place our officers and men had to lay on during the whole siege. Thus it will appear that the 5th Regiment had their share of the hardships and fatigues of the campaign."

The siege ended on August 15—a siege which, "though short in duration, exceeded everything of the sort that ever happened in point of activity and effect during the time it lasted." There was a striking difference between the garrison and our own troops, the former being, with the exception of a regiment or two of French, "the refuse of all nations— a wretched lot. Indeed the island is so unhealthy that Buonaparte never sacrifices his good troops to its baneful effect, but has raised Colonial battalions for the purpose, composed of deserters and all descriptions of vagrants, amongst which number, Irish were the greater part."

The bombardment of the town of Flushing was as complete as engines of destruction could make it, and the way had been made clear for perfect success to attend the expedition ; but all these brilliant endeavours were to prove fruitless. The gross incapacity and indecision of those who were responsible for the campaign turned it into one of our most memorable catastrophes, instead of one of our greatest successes. One of the most magnificent and formidable armaments that had ever left England returned to that country with only part of its original purpose accomplished.

Disease made frightful ravages, and some regiments became altogether ineffective. By the middle of October the sick numbered more than 10,000, and so numerous were the dead that orders were given for them to be buried at night only, and without military honours to either officers or men.

The Fifth, though one of the healthiest regiments in the island, had at one time more than 600 men unfit for duty, and by the beginning of October had lost 3 officers and more than 60 men. Not more than half a dozen officers were at one time fit for duty. From August 21 to December 1, 1809, no fewer than 12,860 sick men were sent home, *exclusive* of those who fell sick and died in the island—"a degree of sickness and mortality unprecedented in any of our unfortunate West India expeditions."

Since the Fifth had by that period suffered heavily in the West Indies, and General Hamilton compared the mortality of the two regions, it will be useful to give the following return of the deaths of the army in the Leeward Islands, part of the West Indies, from March 1, 1796, to the end of the year 1799 :—

Brigadier-Generals	2	Adjutants	11
Lieutenant-Colonels	19	Quartermasters .	9
Majors . .	12	Surgeons . . .	14
Captains. .	72	Assistant-Surgeons	19
Lieutenants . .	109	N.C.O.'s and	
Ensigns . .	60	Privates . .	14,327

About 187 men belonging to drafted regiments, who were left in different general hospitals in July, died in the subsequent months of 1796, and are not included in the above returns. The mortality in that year was most prevalent in St. Lucia and Grenada. The 31st Regiment landed at St. Lucia 775 strong in May; by the latter end of October it had only 16 fit for duty, and by March 1797 had scarcely an officer or man left. The 44th, 48th, and 55th, and York Fusiliers, all strong regiments in May, lost by far the greatest part of their officers and men in the same period. The 27th Regiment lost at Grenada, from June 1796 to February 1797, 20 officers and 516 men; the 57th lost at Grenada, in the same period, 13 officers and 605 men.

CHAPTER VII

THE AFFAIR OF EL BODON

THE Fifth have many Peninsular honours, but they do not include a name—El Bodon—which is as much associated with the regiment as any of the distinctions that have been officially bestowed, and one in all respects worthy of putting side by side with " Wilhelmstahl." Even amongst the brilliant achievements of the regiment at a time when brilliant deeds were expected from our troops as a matter of course, there stands forth prominently the exploit of El Bodon. At that village, near Ciudad Rodrigo, the Fifth, the 77th (now the 2nd Battalion Middlesex Regiment), and a Portuguese regiment held in check a force of 14 battalions of infantry and between 30 and 40 squadrons of cavalry, with 12 guns, and by their bravery elicited from the Duke of Wellington words of praise the like of which he rarely uttered.

On September 24, 1811, the Fifth were ordered to a position on the heights near El Bodon. The enemy, having assembled in very strong force for the relief of Ciudad Rodrigo, advanced on the morning of the 25th, and a furious attack was made on the village. The enemy's horsemen, without waiting for their infantry, began the fight, and a bold dash resulted in the loss of a couple of our guns. "The danger was then imminent," wrote Napier, "when suddenly the 5th Regiment, led by Major Ridge, a daring spirit, darted into the midst of the French cavalry and retook the artillery, which again opened its fire, and nearly at the same time the 77th, supported by the 21st Portuguese, repulsed the enemy on the left. . . . Then the 5th and 77th, two weak battalions formed in one square, were quite exposed, and in an instant the whole of the French cavalry came thundering down upon them. But how vain, how fruitless to match the sword with the musket! to send the charging horseman

against the steadfast veteran[1] The multitudi-
nous squadrons, rending the skies with their
shouts, and closing upon the glowing squares
like the falling edges of a burning crater, were
as instantly rejected, scorched, and scattered
abroad ; and the rolling peal of musketry had
scarcely ceased to echo in the hills, when bayonets
glittered at the edge of the smoke, and with
firm and even step the British regiments came
forth like the holy men from the Assyrian's
furnace."

The Marquis of Londonderry also gave a
stirring description of this affair, so memorable
in the annals of the Fifth. The attack, he
said, was begun by a column of cavalry, which
charged up the heights in gallant style, cheering
in the usual manner of the French, and making
directly for the guns. The artillerymen stood
their ground resolutely, giving their fire to the
last ; but there being nothing immediately at
hand to support them, they were compelled to
retire, and the guns fell for a moment into the
hands of the assailants. But it was only for a
moment, for the Fifth Regiment was ordered

instantly to recover them. They marched up in line, firing with great coolness, and when at the distance of only a few paces from their adversaries, brought their bayonets to the charging position and rushed forward. "This is, I believe," he added, "the first instance on record of the charge of the bayonet being made upon cavalry by infantry in line; nor, perhaps, would it be prudent to introduce the practice. But never was charge more successful. Possessing the advantage of ground, and keeping in close and compact array, the 5th literally pushed their adversaries down the hill, retook the guns, and limbering them to the horses, which had followed their advance, removed them safely."

Wellington, in his public despatch, describes how he had reinforced the Fifth by the 77th Regiment and the 21st Portuguese Regiment and other troops. The small body of defenders had to sustain the attack of the French cavalry and artillery. "One regiment of French dragoons," said Wellington, "succeeded in taking two pieces of cannon, which had been posted on a rising ground on the right of our

LIEUT.-GEN. BRYAN MILMAN, C.B.

(Colonel, Northumberland Fusiliers)

troops; but they were charged by the second battalion of the Fifth Regiment, under the command of Major Ridge, and the guns were immediately retaken." There was plenty more stiff fighting before the British withdrew in perfect order. "The conduct of the second battalion of the Fifth Regiment," . . . continued Wellington, "affords a memorable example of what the steadiness and discipline of the troops, and their confidence in their officers, can effect in the most difficult and trying situations. . . . I have never seen a more determined attack than that made by the whole of the enemy's cavalry, with every advantage of the assistance of a superior artillery, and repulsed by these two weak battalions" (Fifth and 77th). So impressed was Lord Wellington by the courage of the Fifth and other troops on this occasion, that in General Orders he held up their conduct as an example to the whole of the allied forces.

The affair of El Bodon has not been dealt with chronologically; it has been referred to out of its place partly because it stands as an isolated instance, but principally because it formed the best possible opening to a chapter dealing with the work of the Fifth in the Peninsula. What that work was is shown by the list of honours for the Peninsular War, during the whole of which the regiment served, differing in this respect from some corps which shared only in part of the great campaigns under Wellington in Spain and Portugal "Roleia," "Vimiera," "Corunna," "Busaco," "Ciudad Rodrigo," "Badajoz," "Salamanca," "Vittoria," "Nivelle," "Orthes," "Toulouse," and "Peninsula"— these are the distinctions which represent the doings of the Fifth in time of war from 1808 to 1814, and which cause the regiment to be particularly identified with the operations in the Peninsula, just as some other British regiments —the "Old Immortals," late 76th Foot, now the 2nd Battalion West Riding Regiment, for instance—are specially associated with the fight for India.

Time after time the Fifth won praise from Wellington and other distinguished officers for their conduct in this great war, and historians like Napier, the Marquis of Londonderry, and

Alison have recorded in their pages many instances of the valour and devotion of the corps. But it was not from these men and officers of the Fifth alone that the regiment won praise for its work in the Peninsula. The most generous admiration of the appearance and performances of the Fifth was expressed by men who had nothing whatever to do with the regiment, and whose testimony therefore is of special value as proof of the high standing of the Fifth amongst the fine old regiments of Wellington's times. In *Camp and Quarters*, Major Patterson, of the 50th—now the Queen's Own (Royal West Kent Regiment)—wrote in terms of admiration of some of the crack corps of the campaign. "There is," he said, "something in the appearance of many corps not easily defined, but which at once gives to the most inexperienced eye the impression that is usually understood among military men by the term 'crack regiment.' This may be distinguished by an off-handed style of doing things, a smartness of their trim, a neatness and particularity, even to the very polish of their buttons, a sharp, lively step of confidence, a sort of pride in one another, expressed upon their countenance, all of which, both as regards the officers and men, immediately informs you, whatever it is, that their *tout ensemble* breathes the very life and essence of a soldier. So peculiarly are they characterised in this way, that even after the lapse of years, of many a hard campaign, when you would suppose the rough usages of service would tarnish or break them down a little, they still retain the impress ; it seems associated with their 'number' in your mind, beyond the possibility of erasure.

These regiments seem to be handed down as an heirloom from one clever officer to another. I scarcely ever knew an instance to the contrary. Perhaps none could be said to verify these remarks more strictly than the Old Fifth, or Northumberlands (since made Fusiliers). There was an air of warlike spirit about them, retained from past experience when, under Ridge, Mackenzie, Eames, Pratt, and many more, they preserved a reputation acquired in other fields. There was nothing lively in their uniforms,

their facings being a muddy gosling green;
but notwithstanding this, there could not be a
cleaner regiment.   When I knew them there
were three Mackenzies in the corps, one of
whom, a colonel, a remarkably fine officer, was
killed at Corunna, the others, captain and
subaltern of the Light Company, died in the
West Indies."

CHAPTER VIII

THE STORMING OF CIUDAD RODRIGO

THE fortress of Ciudad Rodrigo, which gave to
the Fifth the honour of that name, was invested
by the French on June 11, 1810, and was
surrendered to them on July 10 following.
They held it for six months, then—the allied
forces under Wellington having stormed it—the
fortress fell. With it were 1500 prisoners and
321 pieces of cannon. The allied casualties
during the siege were 9 officers and 217 men
killed, and 84 officers and 1000 men wounded ;
of these 6 officers and 140 men were killed, and
60 officers and 500 men wounded on the night
of the assault alone.

While the fortress was one of the most
difficult of places to invest, the means at
Wellington's disposal for reducing it were

utterly inadequate. It happened about this period that some of the implements which had been furnished for the use of the British troops by British contractors were so bad that rather than use them the soldiers did all they could to get tools of French manufacture. These were at any rate reliable. They had been made for service, whereas the British goods had been manufactured for profit by scoundrelly contractors. The force that was to storm and capture a fortress which seemed impregnable and was held by a well-equipped, courageous, and confident garrison, had neither plentiful nor satisfactory means of working. Their *matériel* was scanty, and it was deficient in quality. Wellington had demanded 1400 cars; he could muster no more than 450. He had not a single mortar, his stock of shells and powder was scanty, and he had only 38 24-pounders and 12 howitzers.

The scarcity of transport had made it possible for only these weapons to be got to the trenches, and they would have stood in need of their due supply of ammunition if 8000 shot had not been found amid the ruins of Almeida. So slow and unwilling were the native carters that they were two days in getting *matériel* over ten miles of flat and excellent road. Yet the carters were so powerful and essential to Wellington that it was dangerous to find fault with them. They took offence readily, and deserted on the slightest pretext. It was fortunate for the English general that in order to meet the difficulty of getting country transport he had had 800 carts made, and these now proved his surest means of bringing ammunition up for the siege.

Wellington calculated that he would need twenty-four days to reduce and capture Ciudad Rodrigo; but the siege lasted only half that time. Yet the task had been carried to completion in spite of heavy drawbacks, such as inexperience both of engineer and soldier, heavy fire from the fortress, and cold, wet weather; but the worst obstacle of all was the disgraceful badness of the cutting tools which had been sent from the Storekeeper-General's office in England. "The profits of the contractor," said Napier bitterly, "seemed to be the only thing respected;

the engineers eagerly sought for French implements, because those provided by England were
useless." Strange irony of warfare, that the
tools which the Frenchmen had made should
be the partial means of their undoing, and of
driving the garrison from its fastness.

As described by Lord Londonderry and in
Jones's *Journal of the Sieges*, Rodrigo stood upon
the brink of a rapid river, surrounded by a
plain destitute of positions, water, or cover for
the troops. It would therefore be necessary,
after driving the garrison within their lines, to
carry out the siege by relays of divisions—in
other words, to keep the main body in canton-
ments on the left bank of the Agueda, whilst
a sufficient force should carry on the works
upon the right bank, the rest relieving them in
turn of duty. The Agueda, though fordable
in dry weather, became impassable after a few
hours' heavy rain ; while, if the rain should last
a few days, it would inevitably sweep away the
only bridge which the besiegers had found
practicable to lay down.

Ciudad Rodrigo was built on a rising ground

on the right bank of the Agueda ; it had a double *enceinte* all round it ; the interior wall was of an old construction, of the height of 32 feet, and was generally of bad masonry, without flanks, and with weak parapets and narrow ramparts. The exterior enclosure was a modern *fausse-braie*, of a low profile, and constructed so far down the slope of the hill as to afford but little cover to the interior wall ; and from the same cause of the rapid descent of the hill the *fausse-braie* itself was very imperfectly covered by its glacis. On the east and south sides there were ravelins to the *fausse-braie*, but in no part was there a covered way, nor were there any counter mines. Without the town, at a distance of 300 yards, were the suburbs ; they were enclosed by a bad earthen retrenchment, hastily thrown up by the Spaniards during the investment of the place in 1810. The French since they had been in possession of Rodrigo had made strong posts of three convents, one on either flank of the suburbs, and one in the centre, and they had also converted into an infantry post the convent of Santa Cruz, situated just beyond the glacis on the north-west angle of the place. The works of the suburbs, therefore, though contemptible in themselves, yet, as supported by these convents, were considered as fully competent to resist a *coup-de-main*. The ground without the place was generally flat and the surface rocky, except on the north side, where there are two hills, called the lesser and the greater Teson ; the one, at 180 yards from the works, rose nearly to the level of the ramparts, and the other, at 600 yards' distance, to the height of 13 feet above them. The soil on these hills was very stony, and during winter water usually rose at the depth of 6 inches below the surface. The French had erected a small redoubt on the highest hill, which, from its situation, prevented any attack on that side till it should be taken. This redoubt was supported by two guns and a howitzer in battery on the top of the fortified convent of St. Francisco, at 400 yards from it, and a large proportion of the artillery of the place was in battery to fire upon the approach from the hill.

By the 17th of the month the siege had advanced so well that the *fausse-braie* was shaken to atoms and two formidable breaches had been made in its main walls. Wellington, wishful to spare the lives of the garrison as well as his own troops, demanded surrender. This being refused, it only remained to carry the place by storm, and Wellington fixed on the night of the 19th for the assault. The attack was to be made by such divisions as should happen to be on duty that day in the trenches, and as these chanced to be the Light and 3rd Divisions, theirs was the duty of carrying the fortress by assault.

The main breach was to be carried by the 3rd Division, consisting of the 5th, 45th, 60th (five companies), 74th, 77th, 83rd, 88th, and 94th Regiments ; the smaller breach was to be stormed by the Light Division, consisting of two battalions of the 52nd, one of the 43rd, two of the 95th, and two of caçadores. The regiments of the 3rd Division were preceded by their light companies, under Major Manners, as a storming party. These companies were to be headed by parties carrying wool-packs and ladders, the former for the purpose of filling up the ditch, and the latter to enable the assailants to mount the wall. To aid this principal attack, a demonstration was to be made on the right by Major O'Toole, of the 95th Rifles, at the head of five companies of that regiment, with the light companies of the 83rd and 94th. At the smaller breach, as at the greater breach, a select party of men were appointed to head their comrades. They consisted of 300 volunteers, under the command of Major Napier, brother of the historian; and they, like the storming party elsewhere, were preceded by the bearers of bags, ladders, and other engines for assault.

Partly with a view to draw the enemy's attention from the breaches, and partly in hope that, during the confusion, an entrance might be obtained by escalade, Pack's Portuguese Brigade received instructions to demonstrate, as soon as the firing should become general, against the outwork of St. Jago and the convent of La Caridad. They were to plant their ladders at the moment when their comrades issued from the trenches, and were to deliver the attack, real or false, as circumstances should direct.

The last clause in these instructions was the most significant of all : "Ciudad Rodrigo must be carried by assault this evening at seven o'clock." The order was imperative, but Wellington knew his men, and neither his judgment nor his confidence was at fault.

Thus far the general plan, the success of which was proved by the result of the storming. Letters written to friends by Ridge himself show what the part of the Fifth was in the assault. The letters were amongst the last he wrote. One dated January 22, 1812, was to John Dewes, Paymaster of the 28th Regiment. "The siege of Ciudad Rodrigo," wrote Ridge, "has terminated gloriously, being carried by assault the 12th night by the Light and Third Division. In this the Young Fifth has played a conspicuous part, being honoured with a separate command in the first instance, with directions to force the gate leading into the ditch, then with the ladders provided for the purpose to scale the walls of the *Fausse Braye*, dislodge the enemy's parties there, and turn the guns which flanked the breach, then to proceed along the *Fausse Braye* until we arrived there, when I was to wait and follow in the rear of General M'Kinnon's Brigade, who were to have carried the breach ; but our business was so rapidly executed that the Brigade had not arrived at the breach, only the 94th of our Brigade, which had also a separate route, had come up when a juncture of the two weak regiments was formed, when the enemy opened a perfect sea of fire, of shell, of grenades, grape, and musquetry, and all the combustible devilment they could collect ; our only alternative which presented itself was to run by force the breach, as in the ditch we could not line. ' Rush ' was the word, and the breach was presently carried by the Fifth and 94th, though I regret to say with very great loss. . . . I have made prize of the Govenor's saddle cloth, which is extremely rich, being crimson velvet edged with beautiful gold lace two and a half inches wide ; his French double-barrelled gun has also fallen to my lot.

Our General of Division had given a very handsome order on the occasion, which I shall enclose a copy of. This business has reduced the Battalion to a very few, but we have a detachment of 130 coming out. . . . The 5th Division are at present sent on garrison at Ciudad Rodrigo, destroying our works and clearing and repairing the breach. I think the expedition with which Ciudad has been taken will astonish both French and English, as it cost Massena 51 days, 16 of which he was bombarding the place. Lord Wellington has done everything in 12. We certainly have been most fortunate in the weather, not having a fall of any kind during the siege, but a continued steady frost."

Extract from Division Orders, Tamorra, 20th January 1812.—By the gallant manner in which the breach was last night carried by storm, the 3rd Division has added much credit to its military reputation, and has rendered itself the most conspicuous corps in the British Army

The Commanding Officers of Regiments will be pleased to communicate to the Officers, non-commissioned Officers, and Soldiers of their respective Corps his high approbation of their gallantry on this occasion, and assure them that he conceives the command of the brave 3rd Division as the greatest honour his Majesty could confer upon him. Lieutenant-Colonel Campbell, commanding the Right Brigade and 94th Regiment, Lieutenant-Colonel Duncan, commanding the 77th Regiment, and Major Ridge, 2nd Battalion 5th Regiment, are particularly entitled to the thanks of the Lieutenant-General, as having led and carried the breach, as is Major Manners, 74th Regiment, who gallantly volunteered for the storming-party, and Captain Milne of the 45th Regiment, for the able support of the attack. . . . The Lieutenant-General promised the Flank Com panics one guinea a man in case they were the first to carry the breach, but as from unforseen circumstances it fell to the lot of the corps already mentioned, this sum, which would have amounted to about £300, will be proportionately divided among the British Regiments of the Division, who will do the Lieutenant-General the honour to drink to the future success of the Division.

The other letter was dated January 24, 1812, but the name of the recipient was omitted from the *United Service Journal*, in which the communication was published :—" My dear ——, I shall give you a copy of the order under which we acted on the night of the 19th, and then its result.

Order

" The 5th Regiment will attack the entrance of the ditch at the junction of the counterscarp with the main wall of the place. Major Sturgeon will show them the point of attack. They must issue from the right of the Convent of Santa Cruz. They must have twelve axes, in order to cut down the gate by which the ditch is entered at the junction of the counterscarp with the body of the place. The 5th Regiment is likewise to have twelve scaling ladders, 25 feet long, and immediately on entering the ditch are to scale the *Fausse Braye*, in order to clear it of the enemy's parties, on their left,

towards the principal breach. It will throw
over any guns it may meet with, and will
proceed along the *Fausse Braye* to the breach
in the *Fausse Braye*, where it will wait until
Major-General M'Kinnon's column has passed
on to the main attack, when it will follow in
its rear.

"This Regiment will make its attack at
ten minutes before seven o'clock. The 77th
Regiment will be in reserve on the right of the
Convent of Santa Cruz."

In the course of this letter the writer said ·
"This order was executed to the entire satisfaction of all our superiors—you may suppose not
less so to mine. But instead of following into the
breach on our arrival at it, General M'Kinnon's
Brigade had not arrived ; the 94th only, which
had also a separate route, came up, and a
junction of the two weak regiments was
formed, supported by the 77th — 150 men !
The enemy, on our halting as directed, opened
a most destructive fire of shells, grenades, and
every kind of combustible devilment he could
bring together. This had the effect of deciding

the step we must take, as our orders said
nothing about going back, and poor Dubourdieu
at the moment observing, 'Major, it is as well
to die in the breach as in the ditch, for here
we cannot live,' the two regiments, as by one
consent, pushed up the breach, almost eating
fire. But the 'Mounseers' liked fighting best
at a distance, and gave us ground, and, taking
General Funk with them, neglected to pull
away the planks they had thrown over the
ditches cut by them across the ramparts, by
which neglect their preparations for defence
were rendered ineffectual. Five and ninety-four
followed them right and left, at the same time
keeping, as well as we could, the centre in
check until the arrival of the intended assailants,
when the town and all was ours, the enemy,
one and all, throwing away their arms and
flying to their holes, where they endeavoured
to conceal themselves until the rage of the
British lion had subsided, but they had already
taken the most effectual means to obtain
mercy—as it was, even here, glorious to see
Britons incapable of slaying unarmed men,

though their lives became forfeit by awaiting the assault with two practicable breaches.

" Besides possession of the fortress, the whole of Massena's battering train has become prize, as well as an immense quantity of light artillery which Marmont brought against us on our retreat after El Bodon. The fortress is so well supplied with warlike stores, that not an article of any kind is wanting, notwithstanding the expenditure during the siege. I have been enabled to complete the whole of our drummers with French brass drums, and more had we wanted them.

" The George and Dragon has nearly disappeared from our King's colour by a shell passing through it, though I trust his spirit is left amongst us. . . . Our loss—poor M'Dougall, killed ; Major Grey, Dubourdieu, Johnson, Wylde, M'Kenzie, Fitzgerald, Fairtlough, Ayshford, Canch, and Volunteer Hilliard, wounded ; 38 men killed and 62 wounded. This includes our losses during the siege as well as in the assault.

" Your poor Light Bobs have suffered—3

killed and 10 badly wounded. The grenadiers are the greatest sufferers   There has been a regular traffic of the plunder, but the brave fellows earned it all."

The successful storming was followed by one of those mad orgies which so greatly marred the capture of the chief fortresses of the Peninsula. When the enemy was broken and was flying, the victorious soldiers followed him from street to street, from house to house, in ungovernable fury. While any fugitive who surrendered was spared, the conquerors ruthlessly put to the sword all who resisted. Houses blazed, churches were despoiled, wine and spirit cellars were ransacked, and every kind of outrage added to the wickedness of that appalling night. Not until the exhausted drunkards sank to sleep and the wounded had been taken into temporary hospitals did something like order reign again in the shattered fortress. When the sad dawn broke fires were dying out, and the pallid light showed up the gutted buildings and the corpse-strewn streets. This was part of the price of victory.

CHAPTER IX

THE ESCALADE OF THE CASTLE

LIKE " Wilhelmstahl," " Badajoz " is an honour of special interest to the Fifth. It was at Badajoz that the regiment led the escalade of the castle —that desperate and splendid feat which Wellington is said to have declared saved his honour and gained him the town ; and it was there that the Fifth lost their commanding officer, Ridge, a man who caused Napier to pen one of his most striking sentences, and whose name cannot be forgotten by the Fifth so long as the regiment holds together. " Ridge fell," said Napier, " and no man died that night with more glory— yet many died and there was much glory."

Badajoz endured the miseries and sufferings of a siege three times in thirteen months. The first siege was in April 1811, by Lord Beresford, who was, however, forced to abandon operations by Soult advancing to the relief of the town. This advance of the French marshal led to the battle of Albuera on May 16. Wellington in person undertook the second siege, which was abandoned on June 10, Soult having again advanced, in combined operation with Marmont's army, from the north. The third siege also was directed by Wellington himself. It began on March 17, 1812, and went on uninterruptedly till April 6, when, after a most desperate defence by the French, the town was stormed and taken.

Badajoz, which had a population of about 16,000, was then a large and fortified town standing upon the left bank of the Guadiana, which varied from 300 to 500 yards in width at that place. The river protected the area it embraced from the British operations. Towards the land side the defences were numerous, prominent amongst them being the Picurina, a strong redoubt, and an old castle which crowned the summit of a hill 120 feet high. These ruins covered a considerable area, and with proper care could have been made very formidable.

But the defences had been neglected, and the castle at that time was deficient even in parapet to shelter guns. Recognising the weakness of this spot, the engineers determined to turn one of their attacks against it, believing that here was one of their best chances of success. On the opposite bank of the river, and in a direct line with the castle, stood the heights of St. Cristoval. Their altitude was little less than that of the castle hill, but from the peculiar formation of the latter, the heights commanded a view of everything that went on within its walls. So that an enemy should be prevented from enjoying this advantage, a square fort, of about 300 feet face, had been built on the heights. This fort was strong and regularly constructed, with a stone scarp 20 feet high, and was able, by reason of the rocky ground on which it stood, to offer a determined resistance. But the means of communication between the heights and the town were not good, being carried on either by a long bridge, which was liable to be enfiladed, or by the more dangerous employment of boats. The second attack, it was determined, should be made against Fort St. Cristoval, and the engineers were sanguine of success for this double assault.

Hopeful as the engineers were, the colossal nature of the task was clearly seen. A determined enemy, a garrison of 3000 men, with excellent artillery and two months' stores and food, was shut up in works which had many natural and artificial advantages. To oust him there were besiegers to the number of 14,000 or 15,000, including 3000 Spaniards and 2000 Portuguese militia ; but against the 150 pieces of artillery in Badajoz and its outworks we could oppose only 40 pieces, including four 10-inch and six 8-inch howitzers. The besiegers had no mortars, and accordingly eight of the howitzers were used as such. Their guns were all of brass, of Portuguese manufacture, and two were 24-pounders and four were 16-pounders. The ordnance was, in a word, both old and inefficient, and in consequence the fire at times was quite useless against the weapons of the garrison. There had been collected, too, but a poor supply of engineers' stores, comprising

3500 entrenching tools, 60,000 sand-bags, 600 gabions, a very few fascines, and a totally inadequate supply of splinter-proof timber and planks.

Wellington, despite the odds against him, was determined to reduce Badajoz, and the work of the second siege began. With intrepid spirit the besiegers paved the way for the assaults, Wellington being all the more anxious to storm and reduce the place because of his unwillingness to risk a battle with a covering and besieging corps combined. Bad as the artillery was, a breach which was considered practicable was made in Fort St. Cristoval. The attempt to force in by escalade was made, and with the utmost gallantry, amid a shower of shell, hand grenades, and other missiles, was continued for an hour. At 1 o'clock in the morning, June 7, it was seen that the assault would not succeed, and the storming party—a mere handful of men, less than 200—retired, with half their number killed or wounded. Undeterred by this evil fortune, preparations were made for a fresh assault, incessant practice being kept up with seven iron guns which had arrived from Lisbon. On June 9 Fort St. Cristoval was stormed for the second time. Again there was a forlorn hope of 25 men, the whole storming party numbering 200; again for a full hour the valiant band strove to take the fort, and not until 40 of the stormers were killed and more than 100 wounded did the survivors withdraw. It was a short, fearful struggle. The ladders by which the stormers mounted were seized and upset, and the swarming soldiers thrown into the ditch. A perfect storm of shells and stones, grenades, and bags of powder and combustibles fell upon the living and the dead, while those intrepid men who fought their way up to the parapet, rung by rung, were instantly bayoneted. The second attempt had been made, it had failed, and the stormers who had tried to take the fort had been almost destroyed. On the 10th there was a short truce to allow of the wounded being removed and the dead buried. By evening, guns and stores were being removed, and on the 12th the siege was raised, at a cost to the allies of 9 officers and 109 men killed, and 25 officers and 342 men wounded and taken prisoners—a total loss of 485.

For the time being Badajoz was left. When Wellington again appeared before the town it was as the victor of Ciudad Rodrigo, and with a much more complete siege-train than he had possessed at the second siege. In March three divisions, under Beresford and Picton, were investing Badajoz, and regardless of the stormy weather which prevailed, were making ready for the downfall of the place. Everything, even the weather, was against the assailants, and it was only by the most splendid exertions that the necessity of retiring from before the place was obviated. On the night of the 24th, Fort Picurina was stormed and carried, after a desperate struggle, by 500 men of the 3rd Division—the division to which the Fifth belonged. The assailants lost four officers and 50 men killed, and 15 officers and 250 men wounded ; but of the garrison of 250 only 34 escaped.

By April 6 a general assault was considered

practicable, and Wellington ordered that assault to be given at ten o'clock that night. Three efforts were to be ·made—to storm two breaches that had been made, and, if possible, escalade the castle. The taking of the castle was the most dangerous part of the task, and this was given to the 3rd Division, under Picton, the breaches being entrusted to the Fourth and Light Divisions respectively. Other efforts were determined on late on the day of the assault.

In perfect silence and the intense darkness of the night the divisions formed at their alarm-posts and moved to the points of attack. Scarcely had the 3rd Division reached the bank of the Rivellas when they were discovered by the garrison of the castle, and from the entire face of the work fire was opened on the assailants. But they were not checked for so much as a moment. They pressed on, reared their ladders against the walls, and began the escalade. Now came the crisis. The garrison's efforts so far had been feeble, but no sooner had the ladders been reared and the stormers assembled under the walls than havoc was wrought amongst them by the descent of enormous stones, huge beams of timber, and loaded shot and cold shot, while at the same time a furious fire of musketry caused fearful slaughter. More ladders were fetched and more stormers mounted, but only to be hurled back or bayoneted when they reached the top. But in spite of everything that told against them the Division triumphed. One ladder held, and the assailants clung to it and leaped from it to the wall; other stormers followed upon other ladders, and the place was gained. Maddened stormers swarmed upon the ramparts, and once there, no power within the garrison could drive them back. The castle fell to the Division, and before that valorous body of assailants the French fled, some who resisted being put to the sword, others laying down their arms and becoming prisoners of war.

"He (Ridge) was killed, but the place was carried," wrote an officer who took part in the storming; and so it was. The example of the commanding officer had inspired the Fifth to perform one of the most dangerous and difficult acts of the storming. The castle was won, and was filled by the 3rd Division, who remained in it till daylight. So impossible did the task of capturing the castle seem, that Philippon, the French commander at Badajoz, when told of the escalade, refused to believe the officer who brought the tidings, and delayed sending help until the English were unquestioned masters of the castle.

Wellington, too, scarcely credited the intelligence. During the whole of the fighting he remained in one position, on a height near some quarries, listening to the crash of the guns, the rattle of the muskets, the cries of the combatants, and the whole hideous din. From time to time his aide-de-camp brought him reports of the fight—how the assault went and how the garrisons were holding out. When at last an officer—Lieutentant Tyler, from Picton's Division — reached him and said the castle was taken, Wellington demanded to know who the bearer was. "Are you certain, sir?" he asked. "I entered the castle with the troops, have just left it, and General Picton is in possession," was the answer. "With how many men?" inquired Wellington. "His division," answered Tyler. Then Wellington commanded the bearer of the tidings to return to Picton instantly and tell him to maintain his position at all hazards. For the time being there was delirious joy of conquest; not till later, when Wellington learned at what a sacrifice the victory had been gained, did his wonted firmness fail. Then he yielded to an overwhelming burst of grief.

To the Fifth the escalade of the castle of Badajoz and the death of Ridge will always remain an inspiring memory. A general impression of the storming has been given, but details which concern the Fifth and their commanding officer must be offered also.

It was at a stage of the assault when success seemed hopeless that Ridge rushed forward, mounted the first of the ladders, and at the same time called upon a gallant young officer of the grenadiers of the regiment—Ensign Canch —and the men to follow. "Canch," cried Ridge, "won't you lead the Fifth?" Instantly the ensign was on the steps of another ladder, his sword shielding his head, and the bayonets of his grenadiers protecting him in clusters on either side. Filled with an inflexible determination to succeed, Canch forced his way up the rungs, and was the first to mount the ramparts. In a few seconds Ridge was at his side, having mounted the adjoining ladder ten yards on his junior's left. The cheering and triumphant troops swarmed after their leaders, the castle was won, and the enemy were forced through the double gate into the town. But a reinforcement came from the French reserve; there was a furious firing through the gate from both sides, and in the moment of the victory which he had so gloriously won, Ridge was slain.

Canch subsequently became fort-major of Edinburgh Castle, and furnished particulars of the assault on Ciudad Rodrigo and Badajoz to Alison for that author's *History of Europe*.

Of Ridge a miniature is preserved in the Officers' Mess. At the foot of it is the inscription, " Lieutenant-Colonel Ridge, 2nd Battalion of the 5th Regiment of Foot, who was killed at the siege of Badajoz."

This escalade of the castle of Badajoz was briefly described by an officer who was amongst the very first to enter the building. His statement, which was accepted as a faithful personal account by an eye-witness, reads like the work of an officer of the Fifth; certainly the description relates almost solely to the doings of the regiment, and the writer says of "our beloved and heroic commander" that he was so near as to be in contact with him at the instant of his fall. Be that as it may, the story of the escalade, as told by this officer, deserves a place in the records of the Fifth. On the evening of April 6, 1812, he says, as soon as it was dark enough to prevent observation from the garrison, the two British brigades of the 3rd Division, composed as follows : the right, of the 45th, 74th, and 88th, under Sir J. Kempt ; the left, of the 2nd Battalion 5th, 77th, 83rd, and 94th, under Colonel Campbell of the 94th, their light companies, and three companies of the 5th Battalion 60th, the whole under Lieutenant-Colonel Williams of the 60th, forming the advance, moved from the ground on which they were encamped, in columns right in front. The Division took a circuitous direction towards the river, and, according to a preconcerted plan, halted on the ground which had been pointed out to them, there to await the arrival of the several divisions and corps at the points allotted to each previous to the general attack. During this halt the brigades were earnestly addressed by their commanders on the duty they had to perform.

On the signal for the general attack, the brigades advanced in the order named. The enemy appeared fully aware of the attack, having commenced, and continuing, to throw fireballs, which completely exposed the advance of the troops, particularly on their arrival at the wet ditch which covered the approach to the castle wall. This ditch was passed by wading or going along the top of the dam which terminated it, and which was so narrow as only to admit of the assailants passing by single files, while the enemy continued to keep up a destructive fire at this point. As soon as this obstacle was surmounted, the light companies and the right brigade, under Kempt, moved to the left towards the principal gate of the town; the left, led by Campbell, advanced direct to that part of the castle wall which had been bombarded the preceding year.

"At this point," the officer continues, "some ladders were reared against the wall by some grenadiers of the 5th, at one of which were Colonel Campbell and Lieutenant-Colonel Ridge, who commanded the 5th Regiment, and at another the officers of the grenadiers of the 5th; Colonel Ridge called to Ensign Canch of the latter to lead at his ladder, and immediately both, at their respective ladders, pushed up, followed by their men, and, having succeeded in gaining the top of the wall, they joined, and found that they mustered strong enough to beat off whatever was immediately opposed to them. The gallant Ridge called out, 'Come on, my lads! let us be the first to seize the Governor,' and dashed on, making his way, with those along with him, over the works which had been raised during the siege, exposed to a heavy fire, by which numbers fell, who were soon replaced by those who followed.

"As the 5th advanced, the enemy retired, leaving in the works a few men, who were killed or taken prisoners. Retiring from the ramparts, the French formed in an open space near the castle·gate. For a short time the firing ceased, and the regiment, headed by their commander, continued to feel their way in the dark, following the ramparts until they came to a passage leading to the centre of the castle, and on advancing a short way a column was observed, which caused a momentary hesitation in our advance. Colonel Ridge, who at the time was reconnoitring another opening, called out, 'Why do you hesitate? Forward!' We again, with the greatest caution, and without firing, continued to advance, and on proceeding a little farther, the enemy were observed. We then commenced firing, which was returned by a volley. At this moment our beloved and heroic commander fell, having received a wound in the breast, which immediately proved fatal. The writer of this was so near as to be in contact with him at the instant of his fall. We left a guard by his honoured remains.

"The regiment continued to advance, keeping up a fire, and being now supported by the other corps who were following them up, the enemy retiring and shutting the gates. The inner gate was forced without much difficulty, but the outer one was found strongly secured. The French, however, had left the wicket open, and kept up a heavy fire on those who attempted to pass it. Colonel Campbell now ordered the men to retire within the inner gate of the castle, and directed the Fifth to form in column facing the gates, and that the other regiments should imitate that formation as they collected. The command of the whole had devolved upon Colonel Campbell, Sir J. Kempt having, as well as Sir Thomas Picton, been wounded in the assault. The regiments remained in this order of formation until a communication of their having possession of the castle was made to the Duke of Wellington, to whom, as we understood, the news of our unexpected success had given the highest satisfaction.

"Having continued formed as above till morning, we received orders to advance into the town, and were cheered by the generous admission of our brave comrades, that Picton and the Third Division had taken Badajoz."

The taking of the castle was signalised by a memorable incident. Lieutenant Macpherson of the 45th, having got possession of the French flag, immediately doffed his own .jacket, and hoisted it on the flagstaff. The officer subsequently presented the captured trophy to Picton.

Badajoz had fallen at last, at a cost to the allied army of 5000 officers and men. The 5000 included 700 Portuguese. In the assault alone 3500 fell, 60 officers and more than 700 men being slain on the spot; 600 officers and men fell in the escalade of San Vincente, as many at the castle, and more than 2000 at the breaches.

" Let any man picture to himself this frightful carnage taking place in a space less than 100 yards square," said Napier. " Let him consider that the slain died not all suddenly nor by one manner of death ; that some perished by steel, some by shot, some by water ; that some were crushed and mangled by heavy weights, some trampled upon, some dashed to atoms by the fiery explosions ; that for hours this destruction was endured without shrinking, and that the town was won at last. . . . No age, no nation, ever sent forth braver troops to battle than those who stormed Badajoz."

The other side to this picture is that spectacle of hell let loose which was witnessed in Badajoz for two days after the town fell. Murder, pillage, intemperance, outrage in every form— these were stopped only on the third day, when Wellington, furious at the continuance of the tumult, marched two fresh divisions into the town and hanged some of the worst offenders on a gallows which had been erected in the great square. That stern example quelled the pillage, and order was restored.

The enemy had suffered a loss of 3500 in prisoners alone, the entire survivors of the garrison being captured, while to the victors there fell large numbers of guns and vast quantities of stores and ammunition. In the siege a tremendous amount of *matériel* was expended. In this were included 2523 barrels of powder, each containing 90 lbs., 31,861 round shot, 1826 common and spherical 5½-inch shells, and 1659 rounds of grape and case shot ; 70,000 sand-bags also were required, 1200 gabions, 700 fascines, and 1570 entrenching tools. In addition, 3500 Spanish dollars were disposed of.

The year 1812, in addition to " Ciudad Rodrigo " and " Badajoz," gave to the Fifth the honour of " Salamanca," the 1st Battalion, which had landed at Lisbon on July 20, taking part in this victory on the 22nd, and losing heavily. The 2nd Battalion was ordered home to fill up its depleted ranks. Wellington showed his appreciation of the work and behaviour of that battalion in General Orders, dated Arcala, July 27, 1812 :—" The Commander of the Forces cannot part with the officers and non-commissioned officers of the 2nd Battalion of the Fifth Regiment without again requesting them to accept his thanks for their uniform good conduct and brilliant and important services since they have been under his command."

At Vittoria, May 16, 1813, the 1st Battalion forded the river, and advancing against the

right of the French army at Margarita and
Hermanded, drove in a superior force of the
enemy in gallant style. Again the Fifth came
in for the warm praise of Wellington; Lieutenant-Colonel Pratt obtained a medal, and
"Vittoria" was added to the honours borne on
the colours. The loss of the regiment in this
stubborn and important battle was exceptionally
severe. "Nivelle" and "Nive" were fresh
honours for the regiment before its fighting
ended for the year 1813. In the succeeding year
"Orthes" and "Toulouse" were added to the
honours, while "Peninsula" covered generally
the series of battles in which the regiment had
given so many of its best lives and striven so
successfully for England.

Peace was restored in Europe for the time,
but the Fifth had no rest from warlike operations.
Both battalions in 1815 were in America, from
which country the 1st Battalion joined the British
Army in Paris, having just missed the battle of
Waterloo. The 2nd returned and went to
Gosport. This battalion was disbanded on
June 24, 1816. In 1819 the regiment, now

reduced to one battalion, went from Portsmouth to the West Indies, returning to England in 1826. So famous was the corps, and such a favourite in the country, that it recruited nearly 500 men in the first eleven months which followed its return from the West Indies. After another spell of service in Ireland, the Fifth proceeded to Gibraltar, where in June and July 1834, 53 members, including 1 officer, 3 women, and 4 children, died of cholera. From this period until 1857 the Fifth enjoyed immunity from war, serving in the Mediterranean, Ireland, and the Far East. In 1857 the Fifth were called upon to take the field again, this time in a country where the regiment had not campaigned, but where it was to win one of its greatest honours—" Lucknow."

CHAPTER X

PART of the price of the cherished honour of "Lucknow" is told on regimental monuments in and near the city. One in the old church-yard of the Residency is to the memory of those of the regiment who fell in the Indian Mutiny campaigns of 1857-58-59. The names are given of six officers and eighty-four non-commissioned officers and men of the 5th Fusiliers who lost their lives in the advance upon Luck now under General Havelock during the defence of the Residency under Sir James Outram, K.C.B., and the subsequent operations at the Alumbagh and at the final capture of Lucknow. The second is at the village of Bagorwah, on the Cawnpore Road, five miles from Lucknow, and is in remembrance of Lieutenant J. Brown and two sergeants and twenty privates who fell during the occupation of the Alumbagh ; while a third memorial is near Havelock's tomb in the Alumbagh to the memory of Lieutenant and Adjutant Edwin Haig, who was killed by a round shot on September 23, 1857. The Fifth, too, have an honoured place on the Havelock statue in Trafalgar Square, London.

The total casualties, however, were 473, for from the date of the regiment's arrival in India till that of embarkation for England 2 sergeants and 25 rank and file were killed in action, 1 sergeant and 32 rank and file died of wounds, 17 sergeants, 3 drummers, and 273 rank and file died of disease, and 120 were invalided to England for wounds or disease.

When the Mutiny broke out the Fifth were at Singapore, and were ordered to India. Calcutta was reached on July 4, and on August 2 a detachment of the regiment was present at the engagement which resulted in the relief of Arrah. The rebels had besieged Arrah, and the British force there was in a very precarious position. It was in this action that the Enfield rifle was first tested in earnest since its introduction to the regiment. The weapon was a great success, the conical bullets causing havoc amongst the enemy. But the Fifth had to fall back on the bayonet before the road was clear to enter Arrah. It was a brilliant victory against overwhelming odds, and though the loss of the Fifth was but slight, yet the success of the expedition was so marked as to call for special commendation from the Government of India and the Commander-in-Chief. Arrah, too, was of special interest to the Fifth, since it was there that the regiment first encountered the Indian rebels, and for the first time in its long career fought on the soil of Hindostan.

This was the beginning of another period of constant fighting and privation for the Fifth. Many were the skirmishes and actions in which the regiment shared, all of them leading up to the great achievement of their campaigning—the relief of Lucknow. That city had been seized by the mutineers, and the garrison, consisting mostly of the 32nd Regiment—now the 1st Battalion Duke of Cornwall's Light Infantry

—was besieged in the Residency in July. On September 21, Nos. 1, 2, 3, 6, and 8 Companies of the Fifth, commanded by Major Simmons, formed the advance of the united force under General Havelock which crossed the Ganges near Cawnpore, and, after being engaged in the actions of Lumglewar and Alumbagh, were part of the force which cut its way through to the relief of the Residency. They continued the defence until the advance of Sir Colin Campbell in the following March. In this second relief Nos. 4 and 7 Companies were under Sir Colin, so that the Fifth have a special claim to the honour of "Lucknow," having shared not only in the defence of the city but also in the relief under Havelock and that by Sir Colin Campbell. The regiment, under the command of Colonel Guy, took part in all the operations before the city, and during the capture, after the second advance of Sir Colin under Major Master (Colonel Guy having command of a brigade), from November 1857 to March 1858. The officers killed during the operations were Major Simmons, Captain L'Estrange, Captain Johnson,

Lieutenant and Adjutant Haig, and Lieutenant
Carter. Three Victoria Crosses were won—by
Private Peter M'Manus, Sergeant Robert Grant,
and Private Patrick M'Hale.

The Oudh Field Force, under the command
of Brigadier-General Havelock, C.B.—Major-
General Outram having, with a magnanimity to
which there is no parallel, waived his rank and
determined to accompany Havelock to Lucknow
as a volunteer—numbered 3179 men of all arms.
This total was made up as follows —

European Infantry . . . .
European Volunteer Cavalry
European Artillery . . .
Sikh Infantry . . . .
Native Irregular Cavalry

3179

This force on September 19 began to cross
the Ganges, and on the 21st the troops advanced,
resolved, whatever the cost might be, to rescue
their comrades and the women and children who
were imprisoned in Lucknow and almost at the
mercy of a cruel foe. That advance was made

under conditions resembling those of many famous marches in which the Fifth had shared in other parts of the world. On the 22nd, for example, they forced their way along, through a deluge of rain, for 20 miles, finding shelter for the night in an enclosed village, where officers and men arrived soaked and weary. On the following day the head of the column entered the large plain which extended in front of the Alumbagh, and there the enemy were discovered in force, posted to cover Lucknow, which lay behind. Now was fought the first general engagement of note in which the Fifth had taken part in India, and in which they bore a splendid share. Not long after the action began the regiment advanced through a marshy plain, and notwithstanding the fire of three batteries, drove the rebels from the Alumbagh and palace, and after capturing five guns pursued the mutineers for a considerable distance towards the Charbagh. Darkness stopped the operations, and the regiment, returning to the ground which had been just won, took up quarters for the night in the Alumbagh. Early in the action Lieutenant Haig was killed by a cannon ball. He was afterwards buried in the Alumbagh gardens.

On September 24 Generals Outram and Havelock, from the flat roof of the Alumbagh palace, from which an extensive view of the surrounding country was obtainable, planned their attack for the following day. From this point also a large number of officers and men of the Field Force witnessed that act of valour which gave to the regiment its first Victoria Cross.

A reconnoitring party of the Fifth, under Lieutenant Brown, had been sent from the Alumbagh to ascertain the depth of a stream which flowed along the British front and close under the enemy's position. This party in advancing, skirmishing, was met by a sharp artillery and musketry fire, but it achieved its object and was returning when the enemy's fire became hotter and more dangerous. Private E. Deveney, who was with the retreating detachment, had a leg shot away by a cannon ball. Noticing the occurrence, and determined that not a man of his little party should fall into the power of the merciless foe, the lieutenant rushed to the assistance of the helpless soldier With him went Corporal R. Grant.   There was now a heavy fire from less than a hundred yards in front, but, regardless of this fusilade, Grant helped Deveney, and having collected and brought back a number of the scattered skirmishers, raised the bleeding soldier from the ground, and carried him safely into the Alum bagh.

The actual relief was effected on September 25. By daybreak the whole force, carrying three days' cooked provisions, was steadily advancing.   The tents, the sick and wounded, the commissariat—all that could impede progress —were left in the Alumbagh enclosure, where a little garrison remained and kept up a gallant defence against furious and repeated assaults of the enemy. To that garrison the Fifth contributed Lieutenant Oldfield, 2 sergeants, 3 corporals, and 65 privates.

In the advance the Right Brigade led the column, and the Fifth led the Right Brigade.

The route to be covered was both difficult and confined, and this added seriously to the heavy task before the relieving body. Before progress could be made there was a fierce duel between the hidden and well-protected guns of the enemy and the exposed weapons of the column; but Maude's battery of Royal Artillery cleared the course, and Major Simmons, of the Fifth, ordered his men to advance. They forged ahead until the time for charging came, then, cheering, they dashed at the mutineers and scattered them. At this stage Captain L'Estrange was struck by a grape shot and mortally wounded. The desperate advance continued, the Fifth fighting their way against the growing opposition of the enemy. The city being reached, there came that sort of fighting which Havelock in one of his despatches compared with the fighting at Buenos Ayres and Saragossa, in the former of which the Fifth had taken part. In the Huzrut Gunge a body of the Fifth assaulted and entered a house, and there captured the regimental colour of the 5th Oudh Irregular Infantry. An officer of the Fifth at once presented it to

Generals Outram and Havelock, who, having inspected the colour, returned it to the captors. The trophy was carried by the Fifth through all the subsequent campaigns, and is still in the possession of the regiment.

Meanwhile the struggle continued. In the fierce fighting at the Kaiser Bagh, Captain Johnson was mortally wounded by a musket ball while leading his company, and there were many other losses before the Fifth, weary, thirsty, and hungry, received the praises of the thankful and delighted garrison, and enjoyed a hard earned but still incomplete triumph.

A distressing circumstance attended the success. While the foremost men of the Fifth were clearing the adjacent courtyards of the enemy some Sepoys were encountered. Being clad and armed like the rebels, the Fifth naturally supposed that they were enemies, and rushed upon them with the bayonet. The Sepoys fell, but something in their looks and cries and actions caused the Fifth to stay their hand. An officer who came up interpreted the words which the soldiers had failed to compre-

hend, and the Fifth, to their grief, learned that the
Sepoys were a remnant of the faithful band of
natives of the Lucknow garrison. In their
eagerness to meet their deliverers they had
pushed out from their entrenchments, and had
suffered death at the hands of friends.

Much had been done, but the relief was not
yet complete. On the morning of the 26th it
was found that part of the relieving force,
consisting of 100 men of the 90th Regiment,
nearly all the wounded, the heavy guns, and a
large number of our ammunition waggons, had
been cut off, and were in a precarious position,
being surrounded by the enemy in a walled
passage in front of the Moti Mahal. The
Fifth, torn from their rest, accompanied by a
portion of the Ferozepore Regiment, marched
to the relief of the beleaguered detachment and
effected a junction with it. The Fifth then
took position in a building known as Martin's
House, and this, with the buildings and out-
houses, they held throughout the day against
the enemy in increased force. When darkness
fell another party of the 78th Highlanders had

arrived, and the removal of the wounded to the Chuttur Munzil Palace began. At three o'clock in the morning advantage was taken of the enemy's silence to get through his posts, and in this way the whole force marched undiscovered to the palace, where the heavy guns and waggons were safely parked in one of the royal gardens. An abortive attack on the rearguard was made by the rebels, who had been aroused too late to prevent the operation from being carried out.

The Fifth fixed their headquarters in the Chuttur Munzil Palace. Finding a large body of Sepoys in a walled garden adjoining that in which the guns were placed, Lieutenant J. Creagh got together a little party of his men, and, rushing upon the rebels, the Fifth almost destroyed them. During the subsequent siege this garden was held as an advanced post.

The wounded, who on the 26th had been sent from Martin's House, were under the guidance of a civilian. He showed a short, safe road, but by an unlucky mistake many of the doolie-bearers left the track and unconsciously proceeded towards the enemy. This they did not discover until, reaching the gateway leading into the Cheenah Bazaar, where on the previous day General Neill had been killed by a musket ball—the general was succeeded in the command of his brigade during the advance by Major Simmons of the Fifth—they were fired upon from the loopholes. Terrified by this discovery of their perilous position, the doolie-bearers turned and fled, leaving the wounded to their fate. The escort who accompanied the doolie-bearers could only defend themselves in a neighbouring house, which was swiftly sur-rounded by the rebels, who set the roof on fire. The case was desperate and seemed hopeless—so hopeless that some of the soldiers proposed that the wounded should be abandoned, and that they should cut their own way back through the enemy.

This terrible suggestion was condemned by some of the troops, and foremost amongst those who repudiated it was Private Peter M'Manus of the Fifth. This valiant Fusilier not only refused to leave the helpless sufferers; he left the shelter and comparative safety of the house, and from their exposed and dangerous position helped to remove to a safe place the wounded officers and men in the doolies. M'Manus and his comrades held the house until the morning of the 27th, when a relieving column came from the Moti Mahal. For this and other acts of valour M'Manus was decorated with the Victoria Cross.

General Havelock, in his despatch dated September 30, said, "I am filled with surprise at the success of the operation which demanded the efforts of 10,000 good troops. The advantage gained has cost us dear. The killed, wounded, and missing, the latter being wounded soldiers who, I much fear—some or all—have fallen into the hands of the merciless foe, amounted up to the evening of the 26th to 535 officers and men."

In Division Orders dated Lucknow Residency, September 26, 1867, Sir James Outram said :—
"The relief of the Lucknow garrison having last night been accomplished by General Havelock and his brave troops, Major-General Sir

J. Outram resumes his position as commander
of the forces. The Major-General heartily
congratulates General Havelock, and the troops
whom that gallant and distinguished officer has
so gloriously led to victory, on their brilliant
success over the hosts that have opposed them
since the army crossed the Ganges on the
19th instant. He sincerely believes that in
the history of warfare British valour was never
more conspicuously displayed than on the 21st
instant at Mungulwura, on the 23rd at Alumbagh, and on the 25th, when his heroic comrades
forced the city bridge and other formidable
obstacles which interrupted their passage to the
position held by the beleaguered garrison. . . .
The Major-General begs to return his most
sincere and heartfelt thanks to the General and
his gallant army for their glorious exertions,
the only acknowledgment of their achievements
which it is in his power to render.

" He would especially note the behaviour of
the 5th Fusiliers and Captain Maude's battery,
who led the column on the 25th instant under a
most murderous fire."

Lucknow had been relieved, but the rebels prevented the garrison and the women and children from being withdrawn. The women and children at the Residency numbered 700, and there were more than 500 sick and wounded; but against this heavy burden it was possible to set off the advantage of plentiful food. The grain in store was enough not only to feed the garrison, increased by 2000 new-comers, but Sir Colin Campbell is stated to have carried away with him 160,000 lbs. of corn when he left the Residency. Danger of imminent starvation, therefore, did not exist. Communication with the Alumbagh was cut off, and Outram had two courses open to him. One was to reinforce the garrison with 300 men, and, leaving everything behind, to retire immediately to the Alumbagh with the remains of the infantry; the other was to occupy an extended position in Lucknow, keeping a force large enough to command supplies of provisions, and to maintain himself even on reduced rations until reinforcements came to his relief. General Outram resolved on the latter course, and disposed his troops with the object of holding the palaces and strong buildings to the south and east of the Residency. The Fifth occupied the Chuttur Munzil Palace, and furnished pickets for the defence of the advanced gardens and posts.

The force which Havelock had led was indeed in Lucknow, but, in the General's own words, since the night of the 26th they had been " more closely blockaded than in Jellalabad. We eat a reduced ration of artillery bullock beef, chupatties, and rice, but tea, coffee, sugar, soap, and candles are unknown luxuries. . . . The enemy fire at us perpetually with guns, mortars, and musketry, but our casualties are not very numerous. . . . We are now daily expecting Sir Colin Campbell. . . . I visit the whole of my posts in the palaces and gardens with my staff on foot daily."

During this siege the Fifth were kept constantly on the alert. To the officers already lost they soon added Major Simmons, who on September 29 was killed by a musket shot while leading his men in a sortie against the enemy. A column of 560 men, which was formed to take the enemy's battery in the position called "Phillips' Garden," near the Cawnpore Road, included Lieutenants Meara, Brown, and Creagh, and Ensign Mason and 100 men of the Fifth. On October 2 the battery was assaulted and captured.

On this occasion Lieutenant Brown was mentioned in despatches, and Private M'Hale was recommended to the notice of Sir James Outram. M'Hale was the first man in at the capture of one of the guns, and in a letter to the officer commanding the Fifth, dated November 4, 1857, the Commander-in-Chief made known his wish that if an opportunity occurred of giving M'Hale promotion he would be glad to learn that it had been awarded to him. M'Hale afterwards, with Private M'Manus, received the Victoria Cross, the two men having been selected by their comrades for the honour, under Rule 13 of the Royal Warrant for the Victoria Cross.

The Fifth, it is true, were quartered in a palace, but their mode of life was not in keeping with their surroundings. The officers lived in the same hall as the men, sleeping, as they slept, on the floor or guard-beds. There were no servants, no change of clothing, no toilet requisites, no bedding—not even soap. Their food was the soldiers' scanty ration of meat, atta (coarse flour), rice, and salt ; but there was a total absence of sugar, wines, and spirits, and the physique of all ranks of the Fifth was affected in consequence. The inmates of the hospital, which was at the Residency, suffered seriously, and many lives were lost which could have been saved if proper food had been available. In the matter of clothing the Fifth were no better off than with respect to food. More than one officer considered himself lucky to be able to buy a pair of half-worn trousers from the men of the Residency garrison, who were comparatively well supplied. Owing to this dearth of raiment Havelock issued an order that the troops were to cut holes, large enough for the head to pass through, in the Hindostani counterpanes which they had found in the native houses, and to wear them as greatcoats on guard and picket. To the same use as clothing, soiled silks of the Palace begums were put—indeed the Fifth in India employed many of the shifts to clothe themselves which the regiment had known in the Peninsula half a century before.

The coming of Sir Colin Campbell was anxiously awaited. It was determined that as soon as he should reach the Secunder-bagh, about three miles from the Residency, the outer wall of the advanced guard of the Palace, in which the enemy had made several breaches, should be blown in by mines previously prepared; that two powerful batteries erected in the enclosure should then open on the insurgents' defences in front; and, after the desired effect had been produced, that the troops should storm two buildings called the Hureen Khana, or Deer House, and the steam-engine house. Mines had been driven under these also. Of these mines Sir James Outram, in his despatch to the Chief of Staff, November 25, 1857, said: "I am aware of no parallel to our series of mines in modern war; 21 shafts, aggregating 200· feet in depth, and 3291 feet of gallery, have been executed. The enemy advanced 20 mines against the palaces and outposts ; of these they exploded three, which caused us loss of life, and two which did no injury ; seven had been blown in, and out of seven others the enemy had been driven, and their galleries taken possession of by our miners."

On November 16, at about 11 A.M., it was ascertained that Sir Colin was operating against the Secunder-bagh, and the explosion of the mines in the garden was ordered. Their action, however, was comparatively feeble, so that the batteries had the double task of completing the demolition of the wall, and prostrating and breaching the works and buildings beyond it. At a quarter-past three the mines at the Hureen Khana were effectively exploded, and at half-past the " Advance " sounded. " It is impossible," wrote Havelock in his despatch, " to describe the enthusiasm with which this signal was received by the troops. Pent up in inaction for upwards of six weeks, and subjected to constant attacks, they felt that the hour of retribution and glorious exertion had returned. Their cheers echoed through the courts of the palace, responsive to the bugle sound, and on they rushed to assured victory. The enemy could nowhere withstand them. In a few moments the whole of the buildings were in our possession, and have since been armed with cannon, and steadily held against all attacks."

On the day following this glorious meeting of the besieged and the relieving forces, the officers and men of the Fifth who had held Lucknow against the mutineers shook hands with their comrades of Nos. 4 and 7 Companies, who were with Sir Colin Campbell. The garrison at Lucknow executed its retreat from the Residency, and the women, the wounded, the state prisoners, and the king's treasure, with all the serviceable guns, having been brought out, the covering force, of which the Fifth, now united, formed part, fell back on the Dilkoosha in presence of the whole force of Oudh, and thence, by a slow retreat, to the Alumbagh plain. Sir Colin continued his route to Cawnpore with the women and children, sick and wounded, and the greater part of the effective garrison of Lucknow, leaving General Outram, with a force

of 4000 men, constituting the First Division
of the redistributed army, to hold Lucknow and
its armed hordes in check until it was possible
to take the city from them.

Sir James Outram scored a little victory at
Guilee on December 22, 1857. Determined to
surprise the enemy, Outram marched in the
early morning wtth 1100 infantry, from 100
to 150 cavalry, and 6 guns. Of this force the
Fifth numbered 400, and in a private letter
from the Camp, Alumbagh, Ensign R. W
Danvers, who during the Mutiny was attached
to the Fifth as interpreter, said : " The Fifth
were as usual, in front, and did all the work,
with the artillery and cavalry." This smart
skirmish ended in the capture of 4 of the enemy's
guns, and 11 tumbrils filled with ammunition
packed for service, elephants, camels, and bullock
waggons, with the loss to the English of only 3
killed and 7 wounded. Danvers, who was wounded
by a shower of grape in charging the guns, was
afterwards accidentally shot on parade in China by
some of his own men. He wrote a large number
of important letters relating to the Mutiny.

From the going of Sir Colin until the assault and capture of Lucknow on March 17, the Fifth had an excessively harassing duty to perform. There was constant turning out to repel threatened attacks, the regiment had to furnish strong pickets, and had to obey frequent calls for escorts for convoys. On March 31 the Fifth marched to Cawnpore, and during the rest of the year were employed in stamping out the rebellion in Oudh.

While Sir Colin was effecting the relief of Lucknow the Fifth suffered a loss which was greatly regretted. This was the disappearance of the drum-major's stick, which was a valued trophy, because it had been taken in action in the Peninsula from the drum-major of a French regiment. The colours of the Fifth and the stick, with those of other regiments, had been placed in charge of a guard of the 88th Regiment, as no men of the Fifth were available. The stick was stolen, as well as the tassels, which were cut from the colours; but the thieves were not discovered.

Early in 1859, when the regiment was at

Allahabad, cholera broke out and carried off 46 men in a few weeks. Later in the year the disease reappeared and 24 men were lost. From January 12, 1858, to August 18, 1860, the Depot sent out to India 16 officers, 3 sergeants, 1 drummer, 10 corporals, and 633 privates. Owing to the heavy casualties in the service companies the regiment fell far below its establishment, and great exertions were made to obtain recruits, at first without much success, but later with better results, for while in four months of 1857 only 52 were got, in 1858 307 were obtained. The total number of recruits for five years was 892.

Before leaving Calcutta for England in March 1860 the Victoria Cross was presented to Sergeant Grant and Private M'Hale. This ceremony took place in presence of the garrison of Fort William. In his letter recommending M'Hale the commanding officer said : " His conduct has won the praise of every officer of his regiment who had seen him in action, and his name has become a household word for gallantry amongst his comrades."

CHAPTER XI

MINOR CAMPAIGNS

In the long life of the Fifth there have been in many odd corners of the world minor campaigns in which the regiment has taken part. For a considerable period after the Indian Mutiny the Fifth were peacefully employed at home and abroad. Twenty years passed before the regiment was called upon for active service ; then the campaigning was in the East, a part of the world in which the Fifth had won their last great honour for the colours.

On October 8, 1878, the 1st Battalion, then stationed at Chakrata, was warned by telegram from the adjutant-general for service in Afghanistan. The message ordered the time-expired men who had left for the port of embarkation on the previous day to be recalled. On the

18th the battalion, consisting of 27 officers, 43 sergeants, 15 drummers, and 690 rank and file, marched for the front, leaving a depot with the women and children under Captain Beamish. On November 7 the battalion reached Lawrence-pore and joined the 1st Brigade, Hassan Abdul Field Force, which became on the 20th the 2nd Brigade, 2nd Division, Peshawur Valley Field Force. While at Jumrood the battalion was employed on convoy duties and working parties, and took part in operations in the Bazaar Valley, a skirmish at Deh Sarrak (March 24, 1879), and an affair against the Mohmunds at Kam Dakka. The battalion returned to India, arriving at Chungi on June 23. The number of deaths during the year in the battalion was 2 officers, 3 sergeants, and 64 rank and file, of whom 2 sergeants and 35 rank and file died of cholera.

In 1880 the battalion took part in the second Afghan campaign in operations near Kam Dakka with a force from Safed Sung, and against several forts, and at Gurdi Khas. This period was marked by a stirring and brilliant little

achievement by members of the regiment. On
May 19, 1880, a force, made up of the headquarters of the Fifth, two guns Royal Artillery,
two guns Mountain Artillery, a detachment of
the Madras Native Infantry, and 120 sabres,
Central India Horse, having crossed the Cabul
River, found about 2000 Afghans holding some
ruined forts and walled enclosures at Besud.
From these the enemy was easily driven, with the
exception of twenty-two men, who, seeing that
their retreat to the hills was cut off, retired to a
little loop-holed tower in a corner of the fort.
As it was out of the question to storm this
refuge, the mountain guns were directed upon the
tower. Three of the defenders rushed out, and,
charging, were met by Colonel Rowland, Captain
Kilgour, Colour-Sergeant Woods, Private Open-
shaw of the Fifth, and Private Longworth of
the 12th Foot (now the Suffolk Regiment).
Woods, closely followed by the captain, dashed
into the tower, and the rest of the defenders
were killed. Brigadier-General Doran, who
commanded, said, in his despatch relating to this
exploit, that " a finer display of courage cannot

Photo by Knight, Aldershot.

LIEUT.-COL. C. G. C. MONEY, C.B.

Commanding 1st Battalion.

well be imagined, and I do not hesitate to say
that it deserves the highest reward valour can
obtain." Both Captain Kilgour and Colour-
Sergeant Woods were recommended for the
Victoria Cross; but this well-earned honour
was denied them. Subsequently Woods received from the hands of Her Majesty, at
Osborne, the Medal for Distinguished Conduct
in the Field, in commemoration of the gallantry
displayed by him at Besud, and the officer
obtained a brevet majority.

The battalion returned to India, and on
November 8 embarked for England. The 2nd
Battalion meanwhile had gone out to India
from England, disembarking at Bombay on
February 4. In 1881 the words " Afghanistan,
1879-80," were permitted to be borne on the
colours The medals for the campaigns of
1878-80 were presented to the battalion at a
full-dress parade at Mullingar on May 10, 1882,
by Mrs. Harkness, wife of Lieutenant-Colonel
Harkness, who was in temporary command
pending the arrival of Lieutenant-Colonel Mac-
donald from India. The territorial system

coming into operation in 1881, the designation of the corps was changed to " The Northumberland Fusiliers," the facings were altered from " bright green " to " white," the colour for English regiments not entitled to wear blue as Royal regiments, and the gold lace of officers from the regimental to the " rose " pattern. The Depot ceased to be the 1st Brigade Depot, being called the 5th Regimental District; and was moved from Berwick-on-Tweed to Newcastle-on-Tyne. In 1886 the 1st Battalion, then in Ireland, was called out (June 1) to assist the civil authorities in quelling riots in Belfast.

The 2nd Battalion took part in the Black Mountain Expedition in 1888. Under orders received on September 2, the battalion—strength, 15 officers and 600 warrant and non-commissioned officers and men—marched from Kil dunna on the 20th to join the Hazara Field Force against the Black Mountain tribes. On arriving at Dilbori the battalion joined the 1st Column under Colonel Sym on September 27. The column advanced on October 4, meeting with slight opposition, to Mana-Ka-Dana, proceeding next day to Chittabutt. That place was reached with difficulty, owing to bad roads. On the 6th the column was engaged at Doda, inflicting severe loss on the enemy, and on the 16th a force under Major W. F. Way attacked and burned the village Saidara, the enemy losing several men. On the 19th the force left for Mana-Ka-Dana, and marched thence to Chirmang, and on the 24th took part in operations against the Parari Syads. On the 26th they marched to Maidan, and advanced next day to Dubrai, in support of a force operating against Thakot, returning on the 30th to Maidan. Forming part of the 1st Column against the Allai country, the battalion was engaged on November 1 with the enemy at Corapher Pass, and occupied Chaila Peak, inflicting severe loss on the enemy. Advancing against Pokal, they destroyed the village and blew up the tower. On the 4th they returned to Maidan, and on the 6th marched to Dilbori, thence to Abbotabad, where the force was broken up, and the battalion returned to India, reaching Rawal Pindi on November 25.

In November 1895 the 1st Battalion furnished a section of 1 sergeant, 2 corporals, and 22 privates for field service in Ashanti, under Captain W. H. Sitwell. The operations of the Special Service Corps in Ashanti were most successful, and the troops who took part in them were subsequently decorated with the Ashanti Star.

The Fifth were represented by the 1st Battalion in the Soudan Campaign, for which "Khartoum" is borne on the colours. In that exceptionally successful campaign the 1st Battalion formed, with the 1st Battalion Grenadier Guards, 2nd Battalion Lancashire Fusiliers, and 2nd Battalion Rifle Brigade, the 2nd Brigade of the Infantry Division of the British troops.

Lieutenant-General Grenfell, commanding the Forces in Egypt, in his despatch described the campaign as one of the most successful ever conducted by a British general against a savage foe, resulting in the capture of Omdurman, the destruction of the Dervish power in the Soudan, and the reopening of the waterway to the Equatorial Provinces. "The concentration of the Army on the Atbara was carried out to the hour, and the arrangements for the transport of the Force to the vicinity of the battlefield were made by the Sirdar and his staff with consummate ability. All difficulties were foreseen and provided for, and from the start of the campaign to its close at Omdurman, operations have been conducted with a precision and completeness which have been beyond all praise, while the skill shown in the advance was equalled by the ability with which the Army was commanded in the field. The Sirdar's admirable disposition of the Force, the accurate fire of the artillery and Maxims, and the steady fire discipline of the infantry, assisted by the gunboats, enabled him to destroy his enemy at long range before the bulk of the British and Egyptian Force came under any severe rifle fire, and to this cause may be attributed the comparatively small list of casualties. Never were greater results achieved at such a trifling cost. . . . As regards the Force employed, I can say with truth that never in the course of my service have I seen a finer body of troops than the British contingent of cavalry, artillery, engineers, and infantry placed at the disposal of the Sirdar as regards physique, smartness, and soldierlike bearing."

The Sirdar, Sir Herbert (afterwards Lord) Kitchener, in his account of the operations, mentioned, amongst others, the following officers and non-commissioned officers of the Fifth who had been brought to his notice for good conduct :—Lieutenant-Colonel C. G. C. Money, Major the Hon. C. Lambton, Major W. H. Sitwell, Major C. E. Keith-Falconer, Captain St. G. C. Henry, Captain and Adjutant G. L. S. Ray, Lieutenant C. M. A. Wood, Colour-Sergeant T. Burdett, Sergeant-Drummer J. Cordeal, and Sergeant A. Bannerman. Lieutenant Wood was the only British officer who accompanied Major Stuart-Wortley and the Friendlies along the eastern bank of the Nile during the advance on Khartoum. On one occasion they were suddenly attacked by about twenty-five Baggara horsemen, who appeared from behind a village. One of these rode at Lieutenant Wood, who fired his revolver, but missed him. The Dervish then hurled his spear at the officer, whom he failed to hit. Again the lieutenant fired, and this time he shot his opponent in the mouth, and knocked him off his horse. For their services at Khartoum Colonel Money was made a Companion of the Most Honourable Order of the Bath, Major Lambton a Companion of the Distinguished Service Order, Major Sitwell and Captain and Brevet-Major Keith-Falconer became brevet lieutenant-colonels, Captain Ray was promoted major, and Burdett, Cordeal, and Bannerman received the Medal for Distinguished Conduct in the Field.

Though the casualties in battle were confined to a few men wounded, yet the battalion suffered considerably from disease, two officers—Second Lieutenants W. A. L. Hale and H. V. Fison— and thirty-two non-commissioned officers and men dying of illness during or contracted in the Soudan Campaign. To their memory a latten brass memorial was unveiled in the north aisle of Newcastle Cathedral on August 25, 1899, by the Duke of Northumberland, K.G., honorary colonel of the 5th Battalion. The brass is nearly under the old colours of the regiment, and close to the Indian Mutiny memorial. The special service was attended by a detachment of the Fifth from the Depot at Newcastle, and was deeply impressive throughout. In withdrawing the banner covering the tablet the Duke solemnly said : "I unveil this memorial brass to the glory of God and in memory of the officers, non-commissioned officers, and men of the 1st Battalion of the 5th Northumberland Fusiliers who died in the Soudan Campaign of 1898 for their Queen and country." The troops then presented arms, and the band, which had taken up a position in front of the pulpit, played the National Anthem. "Blest are the departed who in the Lord are sleeping" was sung by the choir, and at the close of the service the choir and congregation, accompanied by the band, sang, to Sullivan's Jubilee tune, a special hymn dedicated to the Fifth.

CHAPTER XII

AT 10 P.M. on September 8, 1899, the 1st Battalion of the Fifth, then stationed at Aldershot, received the telegram, " Hold Northumberland Fusiliers in readiness to embark for South Africa about 16th." Instantly preparations were made for active service. One of the most striking features of the departure proved to be that, of the 900 odd men of the battalion, only one failed to pass the medical examination as to fitness for the field. When the 1st Battalion had overcome the excitement which was felt upon the receipt of the order, their thoughts turned instantly to the sister battalion, for there were then only two Line battalions of the Fifth, and the satisfaction was complete when it was known that the 2nd Battalion also had been warned to hold itself in readiness for active service.

On Saturday, September 16, the 1st Battalion left Ash Camp Station, Aldershot, for Southampton, where it embarked on the Union liner *Gaul*, a steamer of 4744 tons. Twenty-seven officers, 2 warrant officers, and 781 non-commissioned officers and men embarked. In addition to them the *Gaul* took out several special service officers, three companies of the Army Service Corps, and one of the Army Ordnance Corps.

The officers of the Fifth who embarked were : —Lieutenant-Colonel C. G. C. Money, C.B., commanding ; Majors Hon. C. Lambton, D.S.O., and E. W. Dashwood ; Captains E. B. Eagar, C. H. L. James, Brevet Lieutenant-Colonel C. E. Keith-Falconer, D. Sapte, R. H. Isacke, and S. C. Ferguson ; Lieutenants A. J. B. Percival, C. E. Fishbourne, H. T. Crispin, C. A. Armstrong, F. Bevan, B. T. Buckley, H. S. Toppin, H. G. Lynch-Staunton, R. C. B. Lethbridge, R. W. M. Brine, H. C. Hall, A. C. Girdwood, F. L. Festing, and F. R. Coates ; Second Lieutenants C. Wreford Brown and St.

J. E. Montagu ; Brevet Major and Adjutant
G. L. S. Ray ; Lieutenant and Quartermaster
J. Bett.   Amongst those who saw the regiment
off was Lieutenant-General Bryan Milman, C.B.,
Colonel of the regiment, which he had joined
more than sixty years previously as an ensign.

The men were formed up in companies on
the wharf, and their arms and ordinary kit and
equipment, including their helmets, were passed
from hand to hand to the hold of the *Gaul*,
where they were stored for the voyage.   The
men marched on board with their personal
belongings only—the clothes they were wearing,
their greatcoats, and their sea-kit, which was
carried in a canvas bag.   So smartly was the
embarkation conducted that it was completed in
an hour.   From Aldershot the battalion took
300 rounds of ball ammunition per man and a
machine gun.   The *Gaul* reached Cape Town
on October 7, and on disembarking subsequently,
the Fifth received an enthusiastic welcome.

Exactly seven weeks after the 1st Battalion
left England for the seat of war, the 2nd Battalion,
then stationed at Portsmouth, sailed.   They left

Southampton on Saturday, November 4, in the *Kildonan Castle*, which was then the biggest troopship which had ever left any port in the world. A vessel of 10,000 tons and 11,000 horse-power, she became notable at once, since this was her maiden voyage, and she was converted into a model troopship from a model ocean steamship in the course of three weeks by the incessant labour, night and day, of no fewer than 3000 workmen. When she sailed she carried 99 officers and 2242 men, of whom more than 1700 were accommodated on the main troop-deck alone. Yet there was a place for every soldier and his belongings. Over each man's mess seat was accommodation for his kit, the hammock which by night served as his bed, and a life-belt, in case he should need it. Besides these troops the *Kildonan Castle* carried 5000 revolvers and half a million rounds of Lee-Metford ammunition. A finer and better equipped troopship never sailed from port. The noble vessel justified the expectations held concerning her, for she reached Cape Town at 11 A.M. on November 22.

The total number of the 2nd Battalion on board the vessel was 29 officers and 981 rank and file   The officers were : — Majors G. Frend, in command, W. E. Sturges, and D. S. Stewart ; Captains J. F. Riddell, W. A. Wilmott, E. W. Fletcher, F. G. Casson, Brevet Major and Acting Adjutant A. W. C. Booth, Hon. M. O'Brien, W. Somervell, and F. B. Morley ; Lieutenants J. A. C. Somerville, H. J. C. Rostron, A. W. Rickman, A. M. Gibbes, A. R. Sandilands, A. C. L. H. Jones, H. B. Warwick, J. H. Matthews, H. F. Stobart, L. B. Coulson, A. D. Shafto, and H. J. S. Stanton, and Captain and Quartermaster J. Thomson, with Lieutenants F. W. Radcliffe, of the 2nd Battalion Dorsetshire Regiment, and W. Gowans, of the 1st Battalion Yorkshire Light Infantry, attached for duty.   The troops on board were under the command of Brevet Lieutenant-Colonel S. C. H. Monro, of the 2nd Battalion Seaforth Highlanders, an officer well known to the 2nd Battalion of the Fifth at Rawal Pindi from 1889 to 1893.

There were two exceptional circumstances in

the case of the regiment which, in such strong force, left Great Britain to take part in one of the most difficult and harassing campaigns on record. In the first place nearly all the men were veterans; they had already been on active service; in the second place, the majority were reservists. There were few men who did not possess the Khartoum medal, while of the reservists not one was an absentee. Of the 1st Battalion's total of 810, 619 were reservists, and of the total of 1005 of all ranks of the 2nd Battalion on board the *Kildonan Castle* when she sailed, no fewer than 602 were reservists. Another circumstance worthy of noting is the selection of both battalions for active service. The compliment paid to the corps by the authorities was the greater since both battalions were taken out of their turn.

When the 1st and 2nd Battalions had landed in South Africa there were on active service nearly 2000 officers and men of the Fifth. During the absence of the battalions at the war the colours were taken to the Depot at New-castle-on-Tyne.

CHAPTER XIII

THE FIRST PRICE OF VICTORY

FROM Cape Town the 1st Battalion went by train to Stellenbosch, a rest camp 30 miles to the north, and there received orders to prepare a Mounted Infantry Company of 118 non-commissioned officers and men and 5 officers. Lieutenant-Colonel Keith-Falconer was put in command of this company. Some 50 trained mounted infantry were with the battalion, and the rest were made up by volunteers. Untrained horses and the lack of saddlery were difficulties which had to be overcome in connection with the formation of this mounted section. On October 10 the battalion left Stellenbosch for a destination then unknown, but which proved to be De Aar, the important junction on the Cape Government Railway through which all troops landed in South Africa, except at Durban, had to pass to get to the front On the 18th the battalion went to Orange River, 80 miles up the line, and there joined the garrison, which consisted of a half battalion of the Loyal North Lancashire Regiment, a half battalion Royal Munster Fusiliers, some Engineers, and a detachment of the Royal Artillery, with two guns. Eventually this place was garrisoned by the troops named, the 9th Lancers, and thirteen guns. Orange River, which was a point of importance, was divided into two camps—north and south. The south defended the railway station, and was garrisoned by the Fifth, the Lancers, and the Royal Artillery. The station refreshment-room was used by the officers as a dining, reading, and writing room. For some time the whole battalion was extensively employed on fatigue duties, unloading the heavy trains full of stores that were constantly arriving. But there was soon to be much more serious work than this.

On the afternoon of Wednesday, November 8, Colonel the Hon. G. Gough, who was in command of the troops at Orange River, made a reconnaissance in force, having heard that the Boers were in considerable strength near the camp. The force consisted of the Mounted Infantry Company of the Fifth — 118 men, Lieutenant-Colonel Keith-Falconer in command, with Lieutenants Crispin, Bevan, Toppin, and Hall ; two squadrons 9th Lancers, three field guns, and another company and a half of Mounted Infantry from the Loyal North Lancashire Regiment and the Munster Fusiliers. The single-line railway bridge having been crossed— a tedious and slow proceeding—the little force started for the other side, where it bivouacked. *Reveillé* sounded next morning at four o'clock, and an hour later the troops were searching for the enemy. The Boers' position was supposed to be at Belmont, some 20 miles to the north. After marching till ten o'clock, a halt was made at a large farmhouse near Wittiputs ; the horses were watered and fed, and the officers made the pleasing discovery that the owner had tea and coffee and other good things ready for them. By night the party were back at the farm, having visited Belmont without discovering the Boers.

Early next morning the search was resumed, this time in a slightly different direction. At ten o'clock it was evident that the enemy were about, for some Lancers who had had their horses shot were returning on foot. Hereupon the line of advance was changed almost at right angles, and very soon a puff of smoke from a neighbouring hill indicated hostile artillery. The shells did not burst, but were so well aimed that one fell nearly in the middle of the front squadron of Lancers.

It was now clear that there was to be a smart little brush with the enemy. Not without difficulty the guns were got over a nullah, and the Lancers opened out to the left. The Mounted Infantry galloped off to the right, the guns remaining in the centre. The Boers by this movement were shown to be on the top of a very strong and high ridge of hills, with an extensive front, and with the foe making an admirable target on a perfectly open plain. Despite a very heavy rifle fire the Lancers dashed up in open order to within a thousand yards of the Boers' position. They were lucky enough to escape with the loss of two horses killed. On the right the Mounted Infantry galloped to within 500 yards of the position in the most gallant style. As they rushed forward they dismounted, and now came the time when the Fifth were to make the first of many heavy sacrifices in the war.

Shot through the thigh, so severely that he could not move, Lieutenant Bevan was the first to fall. Seeing the helplessness of his comrade, reckless of personal danger, wishful only to succour and to save, Colonel Keith-Falconer, who was with another section, rose from behind cover to give assistance. His generous courage cost his life, for he instantly fell dead, shot through the side. With a mere handful of men, Lieutenant Hall kept the Boers from getting round the party's flank. He shot three or four of the enemy himself before he was wounded in the thigh, but he was able to ride in. One officer of the Loyal North Lancashire was shot through the head, and two of their men were wounded ; but although a couple of men of the Fifth received bullets through their helmets, not a man or horse of theirs was hit. The dead and wounded were brought in, the Mounted Infantry retiring, covered by the Lancers ; while four companies of the Fifth went out by train just beyond Wittiputs, to cover the retreat of their comrades if necessary. The farm, how-ever, was reached without attack, and a halt of an hour and a half was made for water. About six o'clock the return to Orange River was made, and that place was reached at one o'clock the following morning, after nineteen hours in the saddle.

The reconnaissance had been successful ; the object of the party had been fulfilled. But at what cost? Three out of the five officers of the Fifth killed or wounded. Colonel Keith-Falconer had met a soldier's death ; he was laid in a soldier's grave, a rude but honoured sepulchre in the veldt, with a stone inscribed in white letters :—" Capt. and Bt. Lt.-Col. C. E. Keith-Falconer, 1st Northd. Fusrs., 10th Novr., 1899." He was succeeded by Major Ray—

" Young Ray " he was spoken of affectionately, a brave officer who was soon to follow his superior. He was killed in action at Magersfontein on December 11, 1899, while trying to save a comrade's life. He was at one time editor of the regimental journal, and a sad coincidence was the publication of his last letter in the issue which contained his obituary notice. That number, indeed, was tinged with sadness. It gave a reproduction of a photograph of Colonel Keith-Falconer's grave by an officer— Lieutenant Brine—who by that time was also included in the list of killed. Ray was full of sorrow for his friend. " Poor Keith ! " he wrote in his last letter. "Little did I think when I last wrote to you light-heartedly about the comedy of the campaign that we should so soon be brought face to face with the naked tragedy of it. Yet here we are mourning the loss of as gallant a gentleman and as smart an officer as ever adorned the ranks of the Fifth—killed, too, in a miserable little skirmish."

This honourable but dearly-bought little affair was quickly followed by more serious operations.

CHAPTER XIV

THREE BATTLES IN SIX DAYS

THE 1st Battalion was with the column, 8000 strong, with which Lieut.-General Lord Methuen was to advance without delay from Orange River Station to the relief of Kimberley. When, at dawn on November 21, the advance began, the column consisted of the 9th Lancers, Rimington's Guides, three companies Mounted Infantry, a small Naval Brigade, three field batteries Royal Artillery, the Guards Brigade of four battalions, and the 9th Brigade, also of four battalions. The comrades of the Fifth in the 9th Brigade were the half battalion 1st Loyal North Lancashire (the other half was shut up in Kimberley), the 2nd Northamptonshire Regiment, and the 2nd Yorkshire Light Infantry. In a week the column had won a series of brilliant victories—Belmont, Graspan, and Modder River, and the Fifth, sharing in these triumphs, were amongst the regiments which suffered most severely.

On the 21st the column marched fourteen miles, and on the following day it was found that a Boer force was strongly posted in the hills a few miles east of Belmont Station. A battle was imminent, but the troops were fit and ready for it. Not a man of the Fifth had fallen out, although the heat was intense and they carried rolled greatcoats with all the "oddments" in the pockets. These "oddments" consisted of field cap, flannel shirt, canvas shoes, socks, towel, soap, worsted cap, housewife, laces, and grease-pot, so that the bundle was by no means a light one. At a farm at Belmont the column bivouacked, the troops making themselves snug in blanket *tukûls*.

At dawn on the 22nd, D and E Companies of the Fifth relieved the Scots Guards on outpost duty. Seven or eight miles to the north-east, part of the enemy's position was visible, and Boers were seen moving about. Just before noon the Boers opened fire on some of our cavalry scouts, but the firing was without effect. Early in the afternoon the 9th Lancers, two guns, and a company of the Guards moved off towards Belmont, the rest of the force marching two hours later, and reaching Belmont Farm at 7 P.M. Three Boer guns which opened fire were speedily silenced by our artillery.

It was now Lord Methuen's intention to attack the enemy, if possible by surprise, at dawn on the 23rd, and accordingly a night march was ordered. The column bivouacked until 2.15 A.M., and then started for the enemy's position, which was east of the railway line, very strong among big koppies, and with a front of about two miles. A formidable task awaited the column, even in the most favourable circumstances, and it was made the greater because the Guards Brigade did not reach their rendezvous at the appointed time. This meant that the attack was delayed until daylight The 9th Brigade formed the left, and the Guards the right attack. Of the Fifth the C, D, E, F, G, and H Companies composed the firing line

and supports, and A and B Companies the
reserve. From the railway, across an open
plain, the assailants advanced. The Boers had
the range exactly, and in crossing the line the
force suffered heavily. But the resistless on-
ward movement continued. The first small
koppie was stormed. It was captured. Then
the assailants rushed upon the big one, and
after much firing and struggling, reached the
top, and held it. So furious was the combat
at this stage that the opponents were pouring
fire into each other at a distance of only 50 to
120 yards.

On this shot-stormed summit the Fifth lost
heavily. Captain Eagar, while tending a
wounded man, was shot dead, making the
third officer of the regiment who had given
his life for another within a few days, for Keith-
Falconer and Ray had met their end in the
same nobly unselfish manner. Lieutenant Brine,
while peering over a boulder, was shot through
the head. Major Dashwood, Captain Sapte, and
Lieutenant Fishbourne, with a large number
of men, were wounded at the same place.

Dashwood was shot through the neck and chest, Sapte was shot through the left side, and owed his life to the protection given by his watch; and Fishbourne was struck on the mouth, his jaw being broken. Lieutenant Festing was shot through the chest.

The fight was over at eight o'clock in the morning. When the Fifth began to search for their fallen they learned that 2 officers and 12 men were killed and 37 wounded. In the evening the fourteen were buried in one grave in the north-west corner of the Belmont Farm Cemetery, and on the following morning the Fifth heaped up rocks and earth over the grave, made a big cross, and planted a prickly pear-tree in the centre of their comrades' resting-place.

Amongst the killed and wounded were officers and men who had been struck by several bullets. The wounded included two brothers of the Fifth, each of whom had been hit in the thigh by a bullet.

The total British loss at Belmont was 3 officers and 50 non-commissioned officers and

men killed, and 25 officers and 220 other ranks
wounded, of whom 1 officer and 21 other ranks
died.

After the battle Lord Methuen, addressing
the troops, said :—" Comrades, I congratulate
you on the complete success achieved by you
this morning. The ground over which we
have to fight presents exceptional difficulties,
and we had as an enemy a past master in the
tactics of mounted infantry. With troops such
as you are, a commander can have no fear as to
the result. There is a sad side, and you and
I are thinking as much of those who have died
for the honour of their country and of those
who are suffering as we are thinking of our
victory."

The battle of Enslin, or Graspan, fought on
November 25, meant eleven and a half hours'
fighting, with little to drink and nothing to eat.
The 1st Battalion of the Fifth formed the advanced
guard of the division, and at 3.30 A.M. on the
25th moved from its bivouac at Swinkspan,
7 miles from Belmont, towards Graspan Station.
Although it was not anticipated that there

would be any serious meeting with the enemy
on this day, by half-past seven in the morning
the British artillery was shelling a very strong
position in front, and the Boers were answer-
ing briskly with gun and rifle fire. Five
companies of the Fifth were employed as a
containing force in front of the main position,
while two escorted the guns and one was carried
to the right in a large turning movement to
envelop the left flank of the enemy. This left
flank was most gallantly assaulted by the Naval
Brigade, the Yorkshire Light Infantry, the
Loyal North Lancashire, and the Northampton
Regiments. The assault was successful, but
at a heavy cost. It was possible from this
hill to enfilade the main position, and an incessant fire on the Boers' flank was kept up by the
whole of the 9th Brigade and a force of blue-
jackets and marines. The enemy was compelled
to withdraw, but owing to the poor condition
of our cavalry, effective pursuit was impossible—
a repetition of the drawback which had been
experienced at Belmont. The Naval Brigade
and the Yorkshire Light Infantry suffered very

heavily. In a few minutes the Naval Brigade lost 100 officers and men in killed and wounded, but the Fifth escaped with only 2 men hurt. The brunt of the battle was borne by the 9th Brigade, which on this occasion was commanded by Lieutenant-Colonel Money, 1st Battalion of the Fifth.

The losses at Enslin, according to the table issued by the War Office, were 3 officers and 13 other ranks killed, 6 officers and 163 other ranks wounded, 9 missing. Of the wounded, 4, including 1 officer, died.

Modder River made the third action to be fought in six days. The struggle was a long and desperate one, lasting fourteen hours. The estimated strength of the enemy was 8000. The Boers, established in very strong entrenchments on both sides of the river, were under the direct command of General Cronje. During the day a party of the 9th Brigade got over the river below the enemy's position, turned his right flank, and established themselves on the far bank. They were, unfortunately, shelled by their own as well as the Boer artillery, and forced to halt, but they maintained their position on the far bank. The greater part of the Fifth was engaged in a hot fire fight with the front of the enemy's position. This fire, which began early, lasted until nearly dark. The artillery did admirably, one battery firing close upon 1000 rounds. The party of the Fifth recrossed the river at about 9 P.M. and bivouacked on the southern side, the rest of the battalion being not far away. The whole force crossed the river next day, but during the night the enemy had cleared away, and the victory rested with the column.

For nearly twenty hours the Fifth had nothing but a cup of coffee, and the emergency ration had to be used. The cocoa which was thus obtained proved most acceptable to all ranks. On the day following the engagement the column bivouacked at Modder River Station, and a week's halt was ordered, so that the exhausted troops could recover from the excessive strain which three actions in six days had made upon them. In this battle the Fifth had 13 killed and 31 wounded.

The total casualties at Modder River were 4 officers and 66 other ranks killed, 20 officers and 393 other ranks wounded, of whom 31 died, and 2 were missing. Lord Methuen was amongst the wounded. In his official despatch he referred to the action as " one of the hardest and most trying fights in the annals of the British Army."

CHAPTER XV

So far the record of the Fifth had been brilliant in the war. There had been losses, heavy losses; but while these had been a source of grief both to the regiment and at home, they had been looked upon as one of the inevitable features of a great campaign. There was now to come one of the darkest periods of the operations, two reverses which seemed all the more depressing by contrast with the striking successes which since the war began had been achieved by British arms. It was the fortune of the Fifth to have a share in both these defeats—a trifling share in one, but a much more serious part in the other The 1st Battalion suffered somewhat in the Magersfontein disaster, the 2nd was a victim to the circumstances which resulted in the check at Stormberg.

After the fight at Modder River Methuen's modest force received a great accession in the form of a 4.7 Naval gun, four quick-firing 12-pounders, two howitzer batteries, firing 50-lb. shells, additional cavalry and mounted infantry, etc., and the Highland Brigade, with a half battalion of the Gordon Highlanders extra. The force at Christmas 1899 was composed as follows :—9th and 12th Lancers, the Fifth, Loyal North Lancashire, and Yorkshire Light Infantry Mounted Infantry and Rimington's Scouts ; one 4.7 and four 12-pounder Naval guns, one battery Royal Horse Artillery, the 18th, 62nd, and 75th Batteries Royal Field Artillery, the 37th and 65th Howitzer Batteries, the Guards Brigade, the 9th Brigade, the Highland Brigade, four companies Royal Engineers, one balloon section, ammunition columns, etc.

From the battle of Modder River until December 9 there was little to vary the routine of camp life, a life which was made all the more irritable because of the great heat and the dust and dirt common to the country and the time of year. On that date, however, some excitement was afforded by a night march to the west side of the railway line with the R.H.A. Battery, the 9th Lancers, the Mounted Infantry, and the big 4.7 Naval gun, which had become known as "Our Joey." The force advanced about $1\frac{1}{2}$ mile towards the enemy's position, and, with the object of forcing them to disclose themselves, the Boers were shelled, admirable practice being made with the 4.7 at nearly 7000 yards. The weapon seemed, says the correspondent of the 1st Battalion, "to hit anything it liked to. We saw a good many Boers skipping about; then we skipped home ourselves to breakfast at 7.30 A.M.—to us a novel and charming way of fighting; all the hitting on our side. The wily Boers disclosed nothing."

December 11 was a gloomy day for Methuen's forces. On it was fought the battle of Magersfontein, which cost us 23 officers and 148 other ranks killed, and 45 officers and 647 other ranks wounded, of whom 3 officers and 35 other ranks died. The missing and prisoners numbered 107. In this disastrous attack on the Boer position the Fifth took only a small part, being with the Reserve Brigade guarding the camp and making a demonstration to threaten the Boer right flank. The Mounted Infantry, however, were engaged, and acquitted themselves most honourably. It was here that Captain and Brevet Major G. L. S. Ray was killed while trying to aid a wounded comrade. The koppies at Magersfontein, with a front of 2 miles, and trenches running south-east to the Modder River for another 4 miles, made an immensely strong position. But if the Fifth did not share actively in the fight, officers and men had to undergo severe privations on the veldt for four days and three nights, one of which was bitterly cold and wet—incessant heavy rain, with thunder and lightning. At this period, indeed, one only lived from 5 P.M. to 5 A.M., "the rest of the day being absolute purgatory, owing to the dust, heat, and flies."

Meanwhile, at Stormberg the 2nd Battalion of the Fifth had met with exceptional ill-fortune.

The battalion, after reaching their base, East London, at the end of the voyage from England, had made a twenty hours' railway journey to Puttar's Kraal, where they were met by their general officer commanding, Sir William Gatacre. They were eventually transferred from the lines of communication to the 3rd Division, and were very soon in as perfect fighting trim as any of the troops in South Africa. Their first taste of the war was to be an action in which they furnished something like half of the total casualties suffered by the force engaged.

General Gatacre's intention was to attack Stormberg by surprise at dawn, after a night march. His force was a very small one, consisting only of some 850 mounted infantry and volunteer horsemen, two batteries of field artillery, and three and a half battalions of infantry. It was known from the first that there was great risk in the attempt, but the possession of Stormberg was imperative, and the General was not alone in believing that the effort to be made was justified by circumstances. The risk was great, but the consequences of victory were greater, and accordingly the assault was ordered. A chain of unlucky events brought not success, but heavy failure. To begin with, the troops had a long and harassing march before the scene of action was reached. The veldt and the railway had deprived them of much of that energy and stamina which were essential for the success of the task imposed upon them. There were many telling drawbacks, but the most serious was the incompetence of a guide who had been employed to lead the way to the enemy's position.

When, soon after midnight, the troops began what was supposed to be the last part of their march before coming into actual conflict with the enemy, there was grave reason for suspecting that the guide did not know his way. The General was accordingly placed in a position of great anxiety and peril; but courageously resolving that it was better to advance than retire, he held on. Not until dawn broke was the enemy's position—or his supposed position —pointed out. This was a koppie about two miles off, and the better to approach it the column, in fours, made its way round a group of hills.

In fancied security, the men were marching on, when from some neighbouring koppies a fierce fire at short range assailed them. The time for action had come Recovering from their surprise, the troops sprang over the boulders, and made desperate efforts to storm and capture the impregnable places in which the Boers were hidden. It was in reality the sort of work which the Fifth were called upon to do at Ciudad Rodrigo and Badajoz, except that here they had none of the appliances with which the troops under Wellington were equipped. To reach the enemy ladders were needed, and of these there were none. So stubborn was the attempt, nevertheless, that some of the members of the column actually succeeded in getting within a few yards of a lower line of "scanses," but beyond this they were powerless to go.

Such was the critical situation at the break of day. To add to the gravity of it, our artillery, failing in the imperfect light to see that their comrades of the infantry were so gallantly

ascending, opened fire on the enemy. A de
plorable result of this was that several of the
shells fell short, and wrought mischief in the
ranks of the assailants. At the same time the
artillery fire prevented the Boers from destroying
our infantry entirely.

This hopeless struggle had lasted for about
half an hour, when, as it was clear that the
assailants could do nothing—they could neither
fire nor use the bayonet with prospect of success
—the General ordered a retreat. Sadly, un-
willingly, the troops obeyed. In perfect order
and with the utmost steadiness the assailants
withdrew—so collectedly, indeed, that from
time to time a halt was made for a shot at the
entrenched foe. Everything was in favour of
the Boers and against our own people ; but with
a courage and endurance that make Stormberg
as memorable as if it had been a conquest, and
not a reverse, the troops of all ranks continued
their retirement.

" As an example of our rear-guard skirmishing," wrote the correspondent of the *Times*, " the
performances of the Northumberland Fusiliers

and Irish Rifles could scarcely have been surpassed. Disputing every inch of ground, the
survivors of the ill-fated attack finally gained
a line of low hills which formed a horse-shoe
about 1500 yards west of the scene of their
repulse, and from which the road by which the
column had advanced shortly before was within
easy reach. It was indeed fortunate that this
most excellent rallying-position was at hand.
Whilst a sufficient portion lined the crests and
easily kept the enemy back, the remainder were
re-formed in the rear. Then finally, when
all hope of collecting more men had to be
abandoned, the General gave orders for the
retreat upon Molteno. Fortunate, indeed, was
it at the last moment, before leaving Puttar's
Kraal, Sir William decided to take both batteries
of artillery in place of only one. Had there
been but one battery the entire force must have
fallen into the hands of the enemy."

As it was, more than 600 unwounded men
were made prisoners by the enemy. Most of
these were those who, from utter exhaustion,
had fallen at the foot of the ridge from which

the Boers had opened fire, and, unable to join their comrades in the withdrawal, and those troops being powerless to take them away, became captives.

The total casualties at Stormberg were 31 non-commissioned officers and men killed, 7 officers and 51 other ranks wounded, of whom 1 died, and 13 officers and 620 other ranks missing. The loss of the Fifth was 5 officers and 1 attached missing, 12 men killed, 39 other ranks wounded, 1 of whom died; 322 missing. Of the total casualties for Stormberg —702—considerably more than half—399— were sustained by the Fifth alone.

The missing officers were Major W. E. Sturges, Captain E. W. Fletcher, Captain Morley; Second Lieutenant L. B. Coulson, Second Lieutenant G. R. Wake; Lieutenant Radcliffe, 2nd Battalion Dorsetshire Regiment (attached). These officers were removed to Pretoria, where they remained as prisoners of war for many weeks. They were subsequently joined by Lieutenant Toppin of the 1st Battalion, Lieutenant Stewart of the Indian

Staff Corps, formerly of the 2nd Battalion of the Fifth; and Second Lieutenant Butler, 3rd Durham Light Infantry, attached 2nd Battalion. These captives, with about 130 other officers, all lived together "in a long tin building, set in the middle of a space of ground about 200 by 100 yards in size. This resembles a great fowl run, for it is surrounded by an 8 feet high wire netting, outside which is a formidable high barbed wire entanglement." The men were at Waterval, just outside Pretoria, and there, like the other British prisoners, they suffered severely from disease. Many of the men died in captivity. The rest were set free after a long and tedious imprisonment.

Disastrous as Stormberg was to the Fifth, it had many redeeming features. When the full circumstances of the reverse were known and General Gatacre's report was published, it was seen that several of the officers and men of the regiment had acted so well that they were singled out for special praise. The General said, "I bring the names of Second Lieutenant Duncombe Shafto, No. N.F. 2270 Band-

Sergeant J. Stone, No. N.F. 1989 Colour-Sergeant A. Landen, No. N.F. 3923 Private G. Benson, 2nd Battalion Northumberland Fusiliers, to the notice of the Commander-in-Chief."

CHAPTER XVI

MARCHES AND PRIVATIONS

THE 1st and 2nd Battalions of the Fifth, at all times bound together by the strongest links of comradeship, had suffered heavily in the closing weeks of 1899. Death and disaster had told seriously upon them, and the place of many a gallant officer and soldier was to know him no more. But the spirit of the regiment remained as firm and unbroken as ever, the thinned ranks were closed up, and from the feeding-ground at home more members of the Fifth went forth to take the places of the fallen and the missing. Each battalion felt that the campaign had made a heavy drain upon the corps, and was likely to make a heavier; but one spirit only animated every member, and that was, to be in perfect readiness to answer every call. Battle, disease, misfortune, climate—all at this time tended to make a combination of circumstances of depressing nature ; but the regiment was undismayed by them. There was just the same eagerness to be in action as there had been when the Fifth first landed in South Africa, and it was reckoned evil fortune that after Stormberg there should come a time of what was almost inactivity. It was indeed with both battalions a case of calm succeeding storm.

The New Year opened very quietly. The 1st Battalion remained at Modder River, fort and road making, carrying boxes and baggage, and being otherwise usefully and constantly employed. The life and vigour of the battalions were wonderfully well maintained. The realities of war were tempered by the amenities of peace. There was fishing to be had—the battalion took it ; bathing was possible—the battalion enjoyed it ; sports were considered desirable—the battalion got up a gymkana on New Year's Day, and ushered in with fitting honour 1900. The Boers were plentiful among the koppies with their Mausers and their bullets, but this hard fact did not keep the Fifth from having their live wheelbarrow race, their mule race (300 yards, transport only, bridles only, sticks, no spurs), their dancing competition, their officers' handicap; nor did the battalion forget the outsider, for there was a strangers' race, open to all civilians. Life was made tolerable by the battalion for itself; and the gifts from friends at home did much to make the time pass pleasantly.

The 2nd Battalion early in February returned to the country—Sterkstroom Camp—after a month at the seaside. A concert was given for the widows and orphans of the fallen. A notable feature was a selection of music by the band, which, under the conductorship of Sergeant Hamilton, had been brought to a state of creditable efficiency, in spite of the fact that all but eight of the members had been captured at Stormberg. No Boers were in the immediate neighbourhood, but the battalion longed for the day when they could "pitch their tents and eat their breakfast on the top of Stormberg."

While the 2nd Battalion were at East London

orders were given for the raising of a mounted infantry company for every battalion, but the scheme did not advance very rapidly owing to the scarcity of horses and equipment. At Sterkstroom, however, matters improved, and Captain Casson became leader of the "troop," with Lieutenants Rickman and Barclay as his subalterns. Barclay had just joined the battalion for the first time, arriving with a draft of 300 non-commissioned officers and men from home. Casson and he were soon to pay their highest tribute to the enemy.

Several uneventful weeks passed with both battalions, when General Gatacre dined with the officers of the 2nd Battalion—February 22. On the following day a reconnaissance was made from Sterkstroom Camp towards Stormberg by the artillery and mounted infantry. Captain de Montmorency, V.C., with his scouts, was sent forward to reconnoitre. Leaving his men in a position on a koppie, he went forward with three others, amongst whom was Sergeant Howe of the Fifth, who was attached to the scouts as Signalling Sergeant. Howe was left at the foot of the koppie to hold the horses while the others ascended it. On arriving at the top they were all three shot dead by a party of Boers on the other side, about fifty yards away. Sergeant Howe with great luck escaped unhurt back to the remainder of the scouts. The death of Captain de Montmorency, who had won his Cross in the Soudan, was deeply regretted by all.

Within a week the Fifth lost three more officers, killed in action—Brevet Major Booth, Captain Casson, and Second Lieutenant Barclay. Major Booth was killed at Sanna's Post, near the waterworks, Bloemfontein, on March 31, and Casson and Barclay at Reddersburg on April 4.

At Moster's Hock, or Reddersburg, on April 4, 1900, a body of mounted infantry, composed of the 2nd Battalion Fifth and 2nd Battalion Royal Irish Rifles, engaged a much superior force of the enemy. After a long, hard fight the mounted infantry were compelled to surrender, overwhelmed by numbers. It was a little affair in which the Fifth suffered heavily,

the only two officers of the regiment engaged
being killed. One of the officers who was
present, Second Lieutenant Butler, 3rd Battalion
Durham Light Infantry, attached to the 2nd
Battalion Fifth, gave a short, clear statement of
the affair on his arrival at Pretoria as a prisoner.
His story was that on the morning of April 3,
the second day after leaving Dewetsdorp, their
advanced guard reported clouds of dust on the
right flank, showing mounted troops moving in
a south-westerly direction. Second Lieutenant
Barclay, 5th Fusiliers, went out on the right
flank with a small party, and was met by a
party of Boers, under a white flag, who demanded
surrender, in the cause of humanity, as they
numbered 2200 and 4 guns. The party, having
replied that this was impossible, took up an
entrenched position on hills running east and
west. Barclay rejoined his company, which held
the most eastern part of the position, and was
then sent with six men to occupy the left flank
of the eastern koppie, where the enemy first
made their attack. Here the lieutenant was
mortally wounded, being shot through the head

in the first half-hour's fighting. He was instantly attended by Dr. Horne, of the Australian Ambulance. Shortly after this the Mounted Infantry Company of the Fifth, under Captain Casson, retired about 1000 yards to the next koppie, which was due west, and held by the Mounted Infantry Company of the 2nd Battalion of the Royal Irish Rifles, under Captain Dimsdale. The Irish Rifles were on the right and the Fifth on the left. Dimsdale was on the extreme right, and early in the afternoon he was mortally wounded in the neck and head. On hearing this Captain Casson went over to his assistance, and while either helping or talking to him he was shot dead through the head. Casson had walked from the left under a perfect hail of bullets. This left Second Lieutenant Butler in command of the Mounted Infantry of the Fifth. The enemy was beaten back in the afternoon, but the attack was renewed at dawn, and after four and a half hours' heavy fighting under shell and rifle fire, the koppie was outflanked and cut off from the rest of the position, and surrendered at about 10 A.M. on April 4.

Almost simultaneous with the death of Captain Casson and Lieutenant Barclay was the loss of Major Booth at Sanna's Post. This officer had only recently left the 2nd Battalion at the front to join the 1st, and was appointed to the command of the Mounted Infantry, *vice* the late Brevet Major Ray. He, with two other officers and two men with a Maxim, covered the retreat of Colonel Pilcher from Ladybrand, and kept at bay 500 Boers until that officer was able to take up a strong position. Colonel Pilcher and Booth were old brother officers, the former having served in the Fifth. At the time of this occurrence he was second in command of the 2nd Battalion Bedfordshire Regiment, but on special service in South Africa. At Sanna's Post, too, Lieutenant Hall was again wounded and Lieutenant Toppin taken prisoner, Private Downes was killed, and eleven privates wounded. The missing, who were with the sick convoy, numbered eighteen. Lieutenant Buckley, who was present at Sanna's Post, wrote that apparently Booth, Hall, and Toppin, with some eleven or twelve men, were holding on tenaciously as rear-guard, to let the Mounted Infantry get away. The others retired so slowly that Booth and his party found the enemy coming on so close that they were firing at each other for some time at 200 yards' range. The firing was extremely hot, and Hall was soon knocked over, but not before he had fired more than 200 rounds himself. When Hall recovered he found that the Boers were among them, and that the firing had ceased. Booth was shot while endeavouring to get his handkerchief out, for they had expended all their ammunition. Toppin and Lance-Corporal Raynham were the only men of the party not wounded. Private Downes was killed, and all the rest were taken prisoners. Corporal Sinclair died of wounds on April 2, at Bloemfontein.

After these incidents of warfare quietness again fell upon both battalions. The 1st remained at Boshof Camp, the 2nd at Dewetsdorp, in the Orange Free State. An event with the 2nd was a visit from Captain A. G. Tozer, late of the Fifth, then a Captain in the Queenstown Rifle Volunteers. At this period the correspondent of the 2nd Battalion remarked that they had finished their last bottle of whisky, and for the space of three weeks were " a shining band of irreproachable, if somewhat unwilling, teetotalers." So heavy and constant was the work of digging trenches and making shelters that the same scribe had grave fears as to the effect of evolution upon officers and men of the Fifth. He opined that by the time the battalion left Dewetsdorp they would all be qualified navvies, or develop into prehistoric cave men, and when they got home insist on sleeping in the back garden or the coal cellar.

From Boshof the 1st Battalion went to Lindley Camp, Orange River Colony, and the 2nd marched to Bloemfontein. At that place they soon had the joy of receiving a telegram from Pretoria saying that Lord Roberts had entered the capital and released 3500 prisoners. The good news was greeted with great cheering in camp, and there was much speculation as to whether all the officers and men of the Fifth who had been removed to the Boer capital were amongst the prisoners who had been set free in such dramatic fashion. It was not until the battalion got into Bloemfontein that they had certain news which told them that all their officers and men were again at liberty and had been formed into a provisional battalion to protect the Vereeniging Bridge. The battalion learned that the ex-prisoners, although looking well, appeared somewhat strange in the prison garments, in which they were still clothed.

It was at this stage of the war that the 2nd Battalion correspondent proved an exceptionally sound prophet. "The war in the Orange River Colony," he said, "is practically a thing of the past. As soon as those two 'Will-o'-the-Wisps,' the De Wets, have been captured, there should not be another shot fired. Just at present their liberty is full of threats to all, especially to those who travel by train from here to Kroonstad. It must be confessed that, whatever else they may be, they are good sportsmen, and know how to play a losing game out to the finish." These words were fully verified. For a considerable period De Wet, in the most skilful and successful manner, harassed British troops and evaded capture and destruction, at the same time doing great mischief to his enemy.

To the lot of both battalions a good deal of marching had fallen by this time. From May 14 to June 13 the 1st covered 310 miles, the rate varying from 18 to 4 daily. So much marching about was there by the battalion with the object of relieving every one who might be in distress, that they became known as the Salvation Army and Methuen's Mudcrushers. From July 30 to August 22 the 2nd Battalion marched 265½ miles, the day's total varying from 22 to 4. In fifteen consecutive days, beginning on August 8, the battalion marched 234½ miles, an average of about 15½ miles a day—a striking achievement when it is remembered that during this period the men were often on half rations, snatching food and sleep whenever time allowed, and that each man actually carried a weight of arms, equipment, ammunition, necessaries, and blanket or greatcoat, varying from 35 lbs. to 40 lbs. Despite weariness and sore feet—the soles of the boots were worn to the thickness of brown paper—the men stuck to their task with unflagging determination, and in that way gained not the least of the distinctions which their conduct in the war conferred upon them.

Short though such a distance as 4 miles looks in print, it must not be forgotten that many of these fours were made equal to fourteens, or even more, because of the nature of the ground over which the troops were forced to go. "It was koppies and kloofs, kloofs and koppies, the whole time, drops of 400 feet and climbs of 500 feet, so that the 5 miles passed lightly over by the straight-flying crow, lengthened themselves out into the 12 to 15 for the less mobile, perspiring, foot-slogging, crag-hopping Atkins, particularly when his company happened to be one of the two forming the long, widely-extended line of beaters that stretched from north to south of the long mountain range, and was known as the advanced guard."

One day—August 11—brought a march of exceptional severity—a steady drive through blinding, choking clouds of dust raised by a strong head wind. " Just had to put down our heads and plough through it for 14 of the longest miles ever travelled—mostly over burnt veldt and dusty road. Arrived about 4.30 P.M. at Woolfaardt's Farm in most deplorable condition. Eyes like well-cooked chops—black outside and blood-red in ; faces grimy, hair full of dust, footsore, thirsty, and dog-tired. May we never put in such another day ! " Yet at 3 o'clock next morning they were on the march again— not amid heat and dust, but against a high, chill wind which cut into all ranks like a new-set razor.

So much impressed was he by the marching of the column of which the 2nd Battalion of the Fifth formed part, that Major-General Hart, C.B., commanding, issued a Special Order, dated August 12, 1900, Camp Woolfaardt, Transvaal, in which he said : " I congratulate the troops of the Column upon what they have accomplished so far in this difficult and forced march after an active and clever enemy. Great distances have been got over day by day without waiting for needful food and drink, and in the face of abominable wind and blinding dust. Extreme difficulties have been got over with guns weighing seven tons apiece, and the transport of the Force has been kept going to a degree that beats anything I have seen yet in three wars in South Africa." In Regimental Orders, August 14, the commanding officer made known his appreciation of the way in which the non-commissioned officers and men were " sticking to a very trying march under difficult circumstances "; while on the following day Major-General Hart issued a Special Order stating that he had just received a message from Lord Kitchener, who said he fully appreciated the very good marching of the men under difficulties.

The 5th Brigade, which General Hart commanded, was made up of the 2nd Battalion Fifth, 2nd Battalion Somersetshire Light Infantry, 1st Battalion Derbyshire Regiment, and the 2nd Battalion Royal Dublin Fusiliers. It had harassing and incessant work in its chase after and search for the Boer leader, and had to endure the bitter disappointment of knowing that De Wet had slipped away, and that the whole of the work had to be started afresh. Of the appearance of the 2nd Battalion when there had been much fruitless chasing of De Wet the correspondent wrote : " We are like greyhounds ; . . . our coats no longer fit us, . . . but flap idly against our sides like a sail about a mast."

There was a gleam of hope in the report in mid-August that the Brigade were to march to the relief of Colonel Hore, who, besieged by the enemy a few marches away, was in urgent need of help, his small force having suffered a loss of nearly 100. The march was begun early on the morning of August 16, but after two miles had been covered word came that Hore had been relieved, and a return to camp was made to await orders. These came in the evening, and were to the effect that the Brigade were to march at one o'clock next morning and join Kitchener's force, proceeding with him to Pretoria, *via* Elands River, Rustenburg, etc.

The first part of the march to the captured capital was in keeping with the hardships of this famous and fruitless pursuit—it was "a lawful 20 miles on empty stomachs," inasmuch as the commissariat arrangements had gone wrong. The day was hot and dusty, too. There was hope of rest for the day. Vain longing! At 1 P.M. the "dress" sounded, and half an hour later the troops were pushing ahead again to the west. Soon, in the distance, a helio was seen at work. It flashed out a message from Lord Kitchener ordering them to retrace their steps and spend the night in the camp which had been left that morning, and on the morrow to continue the return and start for Pretoria *via* Krugersdorp. Quite in keeping with the buffeting of the Brigade was next day's leading incident—a veldt fire which made havoc in the officers' lines and destroyed kit that was priceless because it could not be replaced. Some consolation was, however, afforded by the publication that evening of an order from Lord Kitchener, as follows :—

"The Major-General has the pleasure to announce the expression of Lord Kitchener's appreciation of what he calls 'the excellent marching' of this Column, together with the expression of his regret that the efforts of all ranks of this Column have not been crowned with better success as regards the enemy. The Major-General in thanking Lord Kitchener on behalf of the Column for his appreciation of our efforts, has said that we are ready to do it again when there may be a chance of tackling them."

When Krugersdorp was reached four days were spent in refitting, in so far as the scant resources of the place allowed this to be done. Here a little auction was held of gifts by friends at home to officers who had returned to England, and to whom therefore the presents were of no value. That they were welcome to the fighters left behind was proved by the prices paid for the articles—prices greatly in excess of the first cost; in the case of slabs of chocolate, seven times as much. Pretoria was at last reached, and then came a prolonged period of tedious service which made all ranks yearn for the day when the order for home should be given. Apparently this was not to come until long after the anniversary of the departure of the

battalion from England for South Africa—
when the greatest fear of the Fifth was that
the war would be over before they could have
a share in it.

This hope of a speedy return to England
also filled the members of the 1st Battalion,
now that the actual heavy warfare seemed at
an end and there was little to do but struggle
through long rounds of tedious duties and
endure perennial discomforts. For some time
the battalion was at Mafeking Camp, Orange
River Colony ; later it was at Camp Rustenburg,
where occasional excitement was afforded by
skirmishes with the enemy. So far it had not
been the good fortune of the battalions to meet
each other during the campaign.

The 1st Battalion Mounted Infantry Company
reached Pretoria early in June, and was afterwards incessantly "trekking" to and from that
city. In one of its moves the company went
over the actual ground where, twenty years earlier,
a detachment of the 94th Regiment (now 2nd
Battalion Connaught Rangers) were massacred.
Of 9 officers and 248 men who were on their way

to Pretoria, 202, including the commanding officer, were killed or wounded. These victims of Boer treachery were buried in a little cemetery, rude and lonely, where they fell. Strangely enough, the company, in passing this sad spot, were accompanied by the 1st Battalion Connaught Rangers—one of the most dramatic features of many in the short history of the Mounted Infantry Company of the 1st Battalion of the Fifth.

CHAPTER XVII

NOOITGEDACHT

In the closing days of 1900 the Fifth again lost heavily in South Africa. The 2nd Battalion, after a prolonged period of the most harassing duty, suffered another mishap which in some respects resembled Stormberg. As with that event so with the affair at Nooitgedacht—early reports distorted and exaggerated the actual occurrence. At Stormberg the Fifth only abandoned the struggle through sheer physical inability to continue it and because of overwhelming odds and want of ammunition. At Nooitgedacht, too, they held on until the last cartridge had been fired and circumstances compelled acceptance of a merely temporary control by an enemy greatly superior in strength and having every advantage of position.

The story of Nooitgedacht is simple. The scene of the action was a horseshoe-shaped depression in the Magaliesberg range. A couple of posts in the centre of this depression were held by four companies of the 2nd Battalion of the Fifth. General Clements's camp was pitched 1000 yards lower down, at the eastern point of the horseshoe, and Colonel Legge's camp was about 800 yards away. The enemy's object was to make a surprise attack, and by sheer weight of numbers overwhelm the British. At dawn on December 13 General Clements's force was attacked by 2500 Boers. The fight began with an attack by the Boers on the positions at the foot of the hills. The enemy were dressed in khaki, and wore slouched hats with ostrich feathers. It was not until they were within about 40 yards of the British position that they were recognised. They assaulted with the utmost determination, and with an excellent prospect of success, as apparently their plans had been skilfully prepared, and they knew where to employ their strength to the best advantage. A simultaneous attack was made on every company and picket in the nek, the Boers departing from their general practice, and rushing forward in the most reckless manner, waving their arms wildly and yelling.

This furious onslaught was repulsed ; but the Boers managed to get to the top of the Magaliesberg, in spite of the most gallant efforts of the Fifth to keep them back. The Fifth had but four companies to hold the mountain, and these proved inadequate to cope with the great force which the enemy brought to bear against them. They held the koppies until their ammunition was entirely exhausted, then, being defenceless, and a meagre reinforcement of one company from another regiment having failed to reach the top, they were overpowered and held as prisoners. The Fifth had made known their critical position, but the General, believing that they could hold their own, and finding it all but impossible to spare troops, sent only a little reinforcement. When this small band reached the spot where the fight was fiercest the Fifth were still holding out, falling where they stood, struggling to the end. Only when their last cartridge was spent, when it was impossible to get more ammunition, and when they were overwhelmed by numbers, did they surrender. Their stand on the Magaliesberg was one of the noblest episodes of the war, and one of the finest achievements in the history of the regiment.

The Boers followed this success by seizing the northern ledge of the ridge overlooking the camp, which was thus made untenable. A withdrawal now became inevitable, and the transport was inspanned. Though this had to be done under a heavy fire, yet everything, including the guns, was got away, and a second position was taken up at a distance of a mile and a half to the south-east. This was held until the afternoon, when a retirement in the direction of Rietfontein was effected in admirable order. The enemy at this period brought two guns and a Maxim into action for a time, and the British casualties were heavy. The retirement, however, was continued in perfect order, being covered in excellent style by a mere handful — sixty — of the 12th Brigade Mounted Infantry. This little band kept the whole of the Boers at bay, and the 600 or 700 men who formed the withdrawing force were enabled to cover a distance of 20 miles to Rietfontein. Some of the stragglers defended themselves with great success until darkness enabled them to slip away. A little party was on the edge of an enormous precipice in the middle of the nek. Above them were the Boers, who could not, however, see them, and below was a 200-feet abyss. This party watched the fight from start to finish, firing their rifles whenever the chance offered, and in this way causing many casualties amongst the Boers. One man fell over the precipice and was killed.

The loss at Nooitgedacht was heavy—7 officers, including the brave Colonel Legge, who belonged to the 20th Hussars, and 7 wounded, and a considerable number of non-commissioned officers and men. Of the Fifth, Captain Somerville, Lieutenant H. J. S. Stanton, Lieutenant J. E. V. Isaac, Lieutenant A. C. L. H. Jones, and Second Lieutenant G. P. Westmacott were wounded; 15 non-commissioned officers and men were killed, and 68 non-commissioned officers and men were wounded, of whom 2 died. The missing were 8 officers and 333 non-commissioned officers and men; they were, however, prisoners for a very brief period, being released after a detention of a few hours.

By the end of 1900 the Fifth had suffered greatly in the war by fighting and disease. All ranks contributed to the heavy casualty lists. The appended statement shows the number of officers killed and wounded up to the beginning of 1901 :—

Killed.

Lieut. - Colonel Keith
  Falconer.
Major Booth.
Major Ray.
Captain Eagar.
Captain Casson.
Lieutenant Brine.
Lieutenant Stanton (died
  of wounds).
Second Lieutenant Bar-
  clay.

Until the war is ended, complete returns of the losses of the Fifth for their country will not be available. When the new century opened, however, the Fifth had a casualty list equal to about 50 per cent of their numbers at the war. This list was represented by the killed, wounded, and missing alone ; but the total is far greater if the deaths from disease and the invalids sent home are added.

The Fifth have many distinctions arising out of war. Is it to be their melancholy honour to have suffered a heavier total loss in this South African Campaign than any other regiment engaged ?

LIEUT.-COL. THE HON. C. LAMBTON. D S O.

Commanding 2nd Battalion

APPENDIX

I. General Chronology of the Fifth Fusiliers

1674. The regiment was raised during the winter of this year for the Dutch service, and was known as The Irish.

1675. The designation "Irish" was discontinued. The badge of St. George and the Dragon, with the motto *Quo fata vocant* and the Rose and Crown, were assumed by the regiment. The facings were gosling green. (This is the colour to-day, the Fifth being the only regiment in the British Army entitled to wear it.)

1676. Siege of Maestricht, at which the Fifth distinguished themselves. Received from the Prince of Orange a gift of six sheep and a fat ox.

1677. Battle of Mont Cassel, April 11. Regiment behaved gallantly against superior numbers and in spite of difficulties of ground.

1678. Battle of St. Denis. Regiment lost 2 officers and about 50 men killed, 10 officers and more than 100 men wounded. This year the regiment was encamped near the ground where the battle of Waterloo was fought in 1815.

1679. Marched to Grave, where the regiment was employed on garrison duty for four years.

1680. Colonel Wisely drowned while on passage to England.

1684. Encamped near Brussels.

1685. Was on the English establishment for two months.

1686. Returned to Holland.

1688. Accompanied the Prince of Orange to England. Revolution. Placed on the English establishment.

1690. Proceeded to Ireland. Battle of the Boyne.

1691. Skirmish near Castle Cuff. Siege of Athlone. Siege of Limerick. Returned to England.

1692. Went to Flanders. Returned to England.

1693. Expedition to Martinico. Returned to England. Went to Flanders.

1695. Covered the siege of Namur.

1696. Major John Bernardi, of the Fifth, imprisoned for being implicated in a plot to assassinate King William. He remained in confinement for more than thirty years, under a special Act of Parliament.

1697. Returned to England.

1698. Went to Ireland.

1707. Embarked for Portugal.

1709. Battle of Caya. The regiment on this occasion acquired great honour by its valour.

1710. Xeres de los Cabaleros stormed and captured.

1713. Embarked for Gibraltar, where the regiment remained in garrison for fifteen years.

1727. Defence of Gibraltar.

1728. Proceeded to Ireland, and remained there for seven years.

1735. Embarked for England.

1737. Returned to Ireland.

1755. Left Ireland and was quartered in England.

1758. Expedition to the coast of France. The Grenadier Company was the first to land. Destruction of shipping, etc., at St. Maloes. Capture of Cherbourg. Returned to England.

1760. Embarked for Germany. Skirmish at Corbach. Battle of Warbourg. Surprise at Zirenberg. Skirmish at Campen.

1761. Battle of Kirch - Denkern. Affair at Capelnhagen. Skirmish at Eimbeck. Skirmish at Foorwohle.

1762. Battle of Wilhelmstahl. In this action six regiments of French grenadiers surrendered to the Fifth. To show his admiration of the conduct of the regiment Prince Ferdinand of Brunswick presented the colonel with a snuff-box, which is still preserved by the officers. The regiment after this action carried a third colour. This was destroyed by fire in 1833. In place of it the regiment was in 1836 authorised to bear " Wilhelmstahl " on the colours. Skirmishes at Lutterberg and Homburg. Covered the siege of Cassel.

1763. England and Ireland. In the last-named country the regiment remained for ten years.

1767. "Order of Merit" established.

1771. Suppression of disturbances in Ireland.

1774. Embarked at Monkston, near Cork, for Boston. The voyage to America lasted two months.

1775. Affair at Concord and Lexington. Attack on Bunker's Hill.

1776. Went from Boston to Halifax. Reduction of Long Island. Action at White Plains. Capture of Forts Washington and Lee. Reduction of New Jersey.

1777. Expedition to Pennsylvania. Actions at Brandywine Creek and Germantown.

1778. Retreat through the Jerseys. Skirmish at Freehold. Expedition to Little Egg Harbour. Reduction of the Island of St. Lucie. The regiment captured the town of Morne Fortuné, and for this act was granted the privilege of wearing a white plume.

1779-80. In various actions in the West Indies. The regiment returned to England in 1780.

1781. Embarked for Ireland.

1783. Present at the installation of the newly-founded Order of St. Patrick, the Grenadier Company furnishing a Guard of Honour at the cathedral.

1784. The regiment named the "Northumberland" Regiment, in compliment to Earl Percy, who had commanded it for sixteen years, including the whole of the American War of Independence.

1785. Received new colours. The men dined by companies in the barrack-yard at the expense of Earl Percy, lately promoted to the Horse Grenadier Guards.

1787. Proceeded from Ireland to Canada. Remained in the interior for nine years.

1797. Returned to England.

1799. Divided into two battalions of 800 each. Both battalions embarked in September for Holland. Actions of Walmenhuysen, Shoreldam, Egmont-op-Zee, and Winkle. Returned to England.

1800. Proceeded to Gibraltar.

1802. Returned to England on the Peace of Amiens. 2nd Battalion disbanded at Winchester.

1803. 1st Battalion ordered to Guernsey. Returned to England in 1804.

1804. A 2nd Battalion again raised.

1805. 2nd Battalion went to Guernsey, 1st Battalion to Hanover. The left wing of the 1st were wrecked off the Helder, and the officers and men made prisoners by the Dutch.

1806. The right wing, 1st Battalion, returned to England, where it was joined by the left wing, which had been liberated on an exchange of prisoners. 1st Battalion went to South America.

1807. Attack on Buenos Ayres. Both battalions went to Ireland.

1808. 1st Battalion proceeded to Portugal. Battle of Roleia. Battle of Vimiera. Advanced into Spain. Retreated to the coast.

1809. Battle of Corunna. 1st Battalion returned to England and joined the disastrous Walcheren Expedition. Returned to England. Detachment at the battle of Talavera. 2nd Battalion went from Ireland to Portugal.

1810. Battle of Busaco. Lines of Torres Vedras. 1st Battalion went from England to Ireland.

1811-12. 2nd Battalion, affair at Redinha. Battle of Sabugal. Battle of Fuentes d'Onor. Siege of Badajoz. Action at El Bodon. Siege of Ciudad Rodrigo. Storming of Badajoz. Colonel Ridge killed. 1st Battalion went from Ireland to Portugal. Both battalions at the battle of Salamanca. Advance to Madrid. Gallant conduct of Private James Grant. 2nd Battalion returned to England. 1st Battalion retreated from Madrid to Portugal.

1813. 1st Battalion, Battle of Vittoria. Battles of the Pyrenees. Entered France. Battle of Nivelle. Passage of the Nive.

1814. Affair near the Gave d'Oleron. Battle of Orthes. Battle of Toulouse. Embarked for North America. Action near Plattsburg.

1815. Went from America to Flanders in four transports. Just missed the battle of Waterloo. Advanced to Paris, and formed part of the Army of Occupation. 2nd Battalion ordered to Gosport.

1816. 2nd Battalion disbanded.

1818. 1st Battalion returned to England; thence to the West Indies.

1821. Reduced from ten to eight companies. In 1825 the battalion was augmented from eight to ten. Phœbe Hessel, formerly a soldier in the Fifth, died, aged 108 years.

1824. Confirmation of privilege of wearing a distinguishing feather. In 1829 the regiment was authorised to wear a red and white feather, the red uppermost as a special honour, the Army Regulations prescribing a white feather to be worn by the infantry.

1826. Embarked for England.

1827. Went to Ireland.

1830. Good conduct during the Galway Election.

1831. Six companies went to Gibraltar, four remaining in Ireland.

1832. The "Order of Merit" sanctioned.

1833. Colours, including the famous third, destroyed by fire at Gibraltar.

1834. Cholera attacked the garrison at Gibraltar. The deaths in the Fifth numbered fifty-two. The colour of the facings changed to a lively green. Service companies went to Malta.

1835. Correspondence respecting an additional banner. Reserve companies proceeded to England.

1836. Regiment equipped as Fusiliers, and styled the Fifth Regiment of Foot, or Northumberland Fusiliers. "Wilhelmstahl" inscribed on the colours, in lieu of the third colour. New colours presented to the regiment at Malta.

1837. Service companies went to Corfu. Home and foreign stations until 1849.

1850. Both battalions again incorporated.

1851. New colours presented.

1856. The "Order of Merit" finally abolished. The men who had medals were allowed to wear them, but any further distribution of the medals was prohibited. Cross-belt abolished and waist-belt substituted.

1857. Headquarters 1st Battalion went from Mauritius to Hong-Kong, thence to Calcutta on outbreak of Mutiny in India. In April 1860 the battalion was back in Calcutta, having fought in many engagements, shared in the relief of Lucknow, and lost in killed, wounded, died of disease, and invalided 473 officers and other ranks from the date of arrival in India to the date of embarkation for England. During the Mutiny, Sergeant Robert Grant, Private M'Manus, and Private P. M'Hale received the Victoria Cross.

1861. 1st Battalion returned to England.

1863. 2nd Battalion went to Natal from Mauritius.

1864. Received new colours. Presentation made by H.R.H. the Duke of Cambridge, Commander-in-Chief, on the Horse Guards Parade, London. Went to Woolwich, where the regiment helped to rebuild the embankment at Erith, which, by an explosion of about 40 tons of gunpowder, had been hurled into the Thames.

1865. 2nd Battalion to Ireland.

1866. Three companies 2nd Battalion from South Africa to St. Helena.   1st Battalion to India.

1867. 2nd Battalion to England.

1868. The King's crest authorised to be borne on the regimental colours.   At Queenstown there died, aged seventy-six years, Lieutenant W. Randolph Hopkins, who carried the colours of the regiment at Ciudad Rodrigo fifty-six years previously.   He planted the colours on the enemy's fortress amid a storm of shot and shell.   At Badajoz he had a leg shattered by a grape shot.   Home and foreign service till 1872.

1872. Non-commissioned officers and men were permitted to wear grenades on their collars.   The distinction of colours in numerals and chevrons on greatcoats between the 1st and 2nd Battalions was abolished.

1873. Officers permitted to wear feather plume, half red, half white, red uppermost, instead of horse-hair plume, ordered to be worn as a peculiar mark of honour on September 11, 1829.

1874. White tunics for the band abolished.

1876. Furnished Guard of Honour to Her Majesty on her visit to Aldershot.

1878. 1st Battalion marched from Chakrata and joined the 2nd Brigade, 2nd Division, Peshawur Valley Field Force.

1879. Employed while at Jumrood on convoy duties and working parties, and after sharing in several affairs returned to India.

1880. Took part in second Afghan Campaign.

1881. Territorial system introduced. The designation of the Fifth was changed to "The Northumberland Fusiliers." The facings from "bright green" to "white," and the gold lace of officers from the regimental pattern to "rose" pattern. The chevrons of all non-commissioned officers, previously worn in the regiment on both arms, to be worn on the right arm only. The words "Afghanistan, 1878-80," permitted to be borne on the colours.

1882. Appointment of hospital sergeants in India discontinued. 1st Battalion went to Ireland.

1883. The *St. George's Gazette*, the regimental journal of the Fifth, founded. First number published at Mullingar, January 31.

1886. 1st Battalion took part in suppressing riots in Belfast. During August and September the detachment was called out in aid of the civil power no fewer than twenty-five times.

1887. 1st Battalion left Newry to take part in Jubilee Review at Aldershot.

1888. 2nd Battalion took part in Black Mountain Expedition.

1890. Medals for Black Mountain Expedition presented at Gharial.

1891. 1st Battalion formed part of troops lining streets when German Emperor visited London.

1892. Privates Bown and Welsh, 2nd Battalion, awarded Royal Humane Society's medals for trying to save a comrade's life in the Cabul River at Now-shera.

1893. Headquarters and wing 2nd Battalion left Peshawur on December 4 by route march to Sitapur (803 miles), arriving at that station on March 3, 1894.

1894. 1st Battalion furnished the English Guard of Honour to Her Majesty on her visit to Aldershot; also to the German Emperor on his visit there. Wearing of silver grenade on shoulder-cords of mess-jacket officially sanctioned.

1895. 2nd Battalion to Straits Settlements and Singapore. Royal Humane Society's medals presented to Corporal Corbett, Privates M'Vay, Miller, Brown, and Owen for gallantry in saving and trying to save comrades from drowning at Fort Siloso, Singapore. On October 5 the Duke of Cambridge made his final inspection of the Portsmouth garrison as Commander-in-Chief. A curious circumstance of the ceremony was that the three regiments which were together at the relief of Lucknow, the 5th, the 90th Light Infantry, and the Madras Fusiliers, were the only regiments of infantry of the line on this parade.

1896. Detachment of the 1st Battalion was with the Special Service Corps in Ashanti. 1st Battalion, after sixteen years' home service, was moved to Gibraltar. 2nd Battalion, after seventeen years' foreign service, embarked from Singapore for Portland. Of the officers who embarked with it for Bombay in 1880, only two and one warrant-officer returned with it. These three were all that remained of nearly 1000 Fusiliers who sailed from Portsmouth in the *Crocodile* on January 1, 1880. Regiment represented in Dongola Expedition. A feature of the year was the meeting at Gibraltar of both battalions. This was on New Year's Eve.

1897. The Queen accepted a copy of the *St. George's Gazette.* Lieutenant Binny received the Royal Humane Society's medal for attempting to save life at Portland.

1898. 1st Battalion went from Gibraltar to Egypt. Battle of Khartoum.

1899 and 1900. South African War. Both battalions went on active service, and suffered heavily.

Battles of Belmont, Graspan, and Modder River, 1st Battalion. Disaster at Stormberg. 2nd Battalion suffered heavily. Long marches, under most difficult conditions, by the Fifth. The regiment earned frequent and special praise for its marching powers. The old gosling green facings restored. New battalions being added to the army, two—the 3rd and 4th—were added to the Fifth. Fifth suffered heavily at Nooitgedacht.

2. Sieges, Battles, and Campaigns in which the Fifth have taken art with the Losses of the Regiment

(In many cases figures are not available)

Year and Name of Battle, etc.	Killed.		Wounded.		Missing.		Died of Disease.		Losses from all Causes.
	Officers.	N.C.O.'s and Men.	Officers.	N.C.O.'s and Men.	Officers.	N.C.O.'s and Men.	Officers.	N.C.O.'s and Men.	
1676. Maestricht		5	10	100					
1695. Namur									Half the Regiment.

Year and Name of Battle, &c.	Killed.		Wounded.		Missing.		Died of Disease.		Losses from all &c.
	Officers.	N.C.O.'s and Men.	Officers.	N.C.O.'s and Men.	Officers.	N.C.O.'s and Men.	Officers.	N.C.O.'s and Men.	
1709. Caya . . .									
1710. Xeres de los Cabaleros .									
1727. Gibraltar . .									
1758. St. Maloes .									
Cherbourg .									
St. Lunaire .									
1760. ...ch . .	::	I		..					
Warbourg .									
Campen . .									
1761. Kirch - Den- ‹drn									
Capelnhagen.									
Eimbeck . .									
Foorwoh e .									
1762. Wilhelmstahl .									
Lutterberg .									
Casse . .									

	22	8	122	
1775. @d ard				
Lexington				
Bunker's Hill				
1776. Long Island				
White Plains				
Forts Washington and Lee				
1777. New Jersey				
Brandywine				
&c	9		42	
On				
17 8. Freehold				
L ttle Egg Harbour				
Morne Fortuné				
1779-8 o Various actions in the West Indies				
1796. Point Levi, aGa				
1799. Bergen				

Year and Name of Battle, etc.	Killed.		Wounded.		Missing.		Died of ...		Losses from all ...
	Officers.	N.C.O.'s and Men.	Officers.	N.C.O.'s and Men.	Officers.	N.C.O.'s and Men.	Officers.	N.C.O.'s and Men.	
1799. Schorledam .	1	5		4		4			85 (1 ... 47 w., 24 m.)
Egmont-op-Zee				2					
Winkle .									
1807. Buenos Ayres .									
1808. Roleia .		3		1					
Vimiera .									
Talavera .									
Tabuya .									
1809. Corunna .				7					13
Flushing .									
Antwerp .									
1810. Busaco .									
1811. Sabugal .		35	o	60					
Fuentes d'Onor									
El Bodon .									
1812. ... Rod-rigo									

1812. Badajoz	2	17	4	30			
Salamanca		11	8	131			
1813. Vittoria	4	72	4	133			
Pyrenees :							
Nivelle		15	2	112			
Orthes	1	11		33			
1814. Gaved'Oleron		7	2	12	13		
Toulouse (and later)		1					
Plattsburg						293	
1857. Indian Mutiny		60					
Arrah							
Secunderbagh							
Dundiekera							84
1878-79-80. Afghan Campaigns—							
Bazar Valley							
Shergai							
Deh Surruck							
Kam Dakka							
Darunta Gorge							
Besud							
Kama							

Year and Name of Battle, etc.	Killed		Wd.		Missing		Died of Disease.		Losses from all causes.
	Officers.	N.C.O.'s and Men.	Officers.	N.C.O.'s and Men.	Officers.	N.C.O.'s and Men.	Officers.	N.C.O.'s and Men.	
1 88. Gle Kus									
Hazara									
Doda									
Chela-Crag									
9_. Asanti Expedition									
1898. Khartoum Expedition								3	
18_. South African Campaign—									
Belmont	2	12		37					
Graspan				2					
Modder River	1	13		31					
Magersfontein	1	12							
Stormberg				39		322			
Reddersberg	2	1			2				
Sanna's Post	1			11					
Nooitgedacht		15	6	68	8	333			

3. Nicknames of the Regiment

"The Old and Bold," by reason of the long and gallant conduct of the Fifth in war.

"The Fighting Fifth," from a favourite saying of Wellington—the "Ever-fighting, Never-failing Fifth"—in connection with the services of the regiment in the Peninsula.

"Lord Wellington's Bodyguard," arising out of the constant association of the Fifth with Wellington. In 1811 the Fifth were attached to headquarters.

"The Shiners," commemorating the cleanliness and smartness of the regiment. This nickname originated in Ireland about 1770.

4. Bibliography

"Military Memoirs. Captain George Carleton." 1728. Reprinted in 1741 under the title of "History of the Last Two Wars," and in 1743 as "Memoirs of Captain George Carleton." New Edition, 1808.

"A Short History of the Life of Major John Bernardi," formerly an Officer of the Fifth. 1729. "Written by himself in Newgate, where he has been for near thirty-three years a Prisoner of State, without any Allowance from the Government, and could never be admitted to his Tryal." Printed for the benefit of the author.

"A System for the Complete Interior Management and Economy of a Battalion of Infantry." Dedicated to Lieutenant-General Studholme Hodgson, Colonel of the 5th Foot. Lieutenant Bennet Cuthbertson, Regimental Adjutant. 1750.

"An Account of the Fifth, or Northumberland Regiment of Foot." The British Military Library, December 1799.

"Historical Record of the Fifth Regiment of Foot." Richard Cannon. 1838.

"Memoirs of a Sergeant of the Fifth Regiment of Foot, containing an account of his service in Hanover, South America, and the Peninsula." 1842. (The British Museum copy contains a M.S. note, dated December 18, 1890, by Captain (now Lieutenant-Colonel) Money, identifying the author as Sergeant Stephen Morley.)

"A Short Narrative of the Regiment." London, 1873.

"Standing Orders." Old Brompton, 1879.

(Second Battalion) "Standing Orders." Chatham, 1882.

"The Standing Orders of the First Battalion Northumberland Fusiliers [5th Regiment of Foot]." 1st May 1895.

"The Whitefoord Papers." Edited, with Introduction and Notes, by W. A. S. Hewins, M.A., Oxford. 1898.

Many valuable manuscripts by members of the regiment, mostly officers, relating to the Fifth on active service and in time of peace, are included in the volumes of the *St. George's Gazette.*

5. EXTRACT FROM "A SHORT HISTORY OF THE LIFE OF MAJOR JOHN BERNARDI," p. 4.

Bernardi's father having removed from Windsor into Worcestershire, to be "more remote and unknown," "his son John arriving to the thirteenth Year of his Age, began to entertain Thoughts of getting from under his Father's Discipline, whose severe Corrections, in the said young Rover's Eyes, had the Appearance of too great Severity, particularly in confining him sometimes like a Criminal in a little Dark Room or Dungeon for Trifles, allowing him only Bread and small Beer for several Days, whilst so confined, and Nobody durst relieve or let him out until his Father gave Order for it. Thus the said John was unhappily destined to Confinement in his Youth by an unkind Father, and in his Old Age to undergo the like rigid Fate by unprecedented Acts of Parliament, without ever being Heard or proved Criminal by any Court in the Kingdom. . . ."

6. EXTRACT FROM "CUTHBERTSON'S SYSTEM, FOR THE COMPLETE INTERIOR MANAGEMENT AND ŒCONOMY OF A BATTALION OF INFANTRY."

Chap. XVI.

Of Courts-martial (*sic*) and Punishments, and the Establishment of an Order of Merit. Art. xxiv.

" To render the necessity of applying to Court-martials (*sic*) less frequent, and to form a Battalion on principles which must produce the happiest effects, an order of merit is recommended for the Non-commission-officers, Drummers, and Private Men ; by which the deserving Soldier will be encouraged to persevere in those paths which led him to the enjoyment of so public a testimony of his Officers' approbation ; and the vicious idle one may be likewise tempted to imitate that conduct which gained the other such applause ; a number of years (not less than seven) employed in the closest attention to military duty, and never in that space having incurred the censure of a Court-martial, should entitle a soldier to the honour of receiving at the head of the Regiment, from the hand of the Commanding Officer, a metal medal, of the size of half a crown, to hang by a ribband from a button of his lapel, in the most conspicuous part ; on one side of which the device or number of the Regiment to be raised, and on the reverse the words, SEVEN YEARS' MILITARY MERIT, encircled in a wreath of laurels ; and as that passion for applause, so natural to mankind in every condition of life, may create a desire in even the most profligate to be some time or other entitled to wear such an honourable badge, they should by no means be excluded from it, if by changing from their former courses they attained to the prescribed number of years established for the order. The greatest strictness must be observed in never conferring this medal on any person without having completed his time of service to a day, and that without the smallest suspicion to the prejudice of his character, because if once a deviation from the original design is countenanced, the order of course must sink in the esteem of the Soldiers, and will no longer answer the purpose of its establishment. It must also be observed, when a Soldier by misconduct forfeits his pretensions of being longer enrolled among the Men of Merit, that his Medal be taken from him by the Drum-major, in the same public manner it was given to him. . . ."

NOTE.—As the "Order of Merit" was not established in the Fifth until 1767, it seems probable that the introduction of the reward was due to the advocacy of Cuthbertson.

7. EXTRACT FROM THE STANDING ORDERS OF THE 1ST BATTALION[1]

Section IX.—The Colours.

5. On St. George's Day the Regimental Colours will be decorated with roses, and trooped, and the Officers and men will wear roses in their caps.

INDEX

Printed by R. & R. CLARK, LIMITED, *Edinburgh.*

Printed in Great Britain
by Amazon